Your Step-by-Step Plan to Look and Feel
Better Than Before

LONG LIVE YOU!

JANE WILKENS MICHAEL

SpryPublishing
ideas to life

This edition is published by
Spry Publishing LLC
315 East Eisenhower Parkway
Suite 2
Ann Arbor, MI 48108 USA

Printed and bound in the United States of America.

10 9 8 7 6 5 4 3 2 1

Library of Congress Control Number: 2014950379

Paperback ISBN: 978-1-938170-52-2
E-book ISBN: 978-1-938170-53-9

Disclaimer: Spry Publishing LLC does not assume responsibility for the contents or opinions expressed herein. Although every precaution is taken to ensure that information is accurate as of the date of publication, differences of opinion exist. The opinions expressed herein are those of the author and do not necessarily reflect the views of the publisher. The information contained in this book is not intended to replace professional advisement of an individual's doctor prior to beginning or changing an individual's course of treatment.

Contents

I dedicate this book to the loves of my life, my three children, Alex, Philip, and Elise, and my daughters-in-law, Molly and Michelle. You all never cease to amaze me. To my beloved twins, Aliza and Zoey, who bring their "Glammy" such new-found joy. And to my true love, The Lawyer, what can I say? Without you nothing would be possible—including this book!

A special word, too, to the courageous cancer survivors who inspired me to work with them in developing a Ladder to the Quality of Life they so deserve.

Finally, I would like to give a special acknowledgment to my mother, Emily, who gave me the wisdom and know-how to write this book. I think about you and miss you every single day. You always encouraged me to fully embrace life and go confidently in the direction of my dreams. I have hitched my wagon to a star—you! And the heavens shine infinitely brighter from your light. You continue to advise and guide me up my own ladder from above. Momma, this one's for you!

Nine Rungs That Can Change Your Life

"If you want to view paradise, simply look around and view it. Anything you want to do, do it. Want to change the world, there's nothing to it."
                                        —Willy Wonka

Years ago, a fortune teller predicted that one day I would be responsible for helping the world become a better place. Of course, she also told me that in a past life I had been a unicorn—so I understandably didn't put much credence in her forecast. Besides, I figured I was already helping others in my own small way. At the time, I was the "Beauty Talk" columnist for *Town & Country* magazine. My columns, though, were not just about glitz and (24-carat) glitter. I tried through my writing to convince my readers that they could shape their own destiny.

I urged readers to follow the example of iconic designer Coco Chanel, who had once said, "My life didn't please me, so I created a new life." In other words, to accept the idea that if they felt unhappy, personally or professionally, it was up to them to make a change. But to do so, they needed to delve deep down into their psyches to find out what they really wanted to accomplish—and then think of ways to go about achieving it. Self-esteem played a huge part. I advised them to believe that true beauty was really all about being comfortable in your own skin—although it never hurt to add a killer coral lipstick!

To backtrack a bit, my knowledge of beauty and health came from my amazing mother, Emily, who was always way ahead of her time. We ate organic before organic was cool (and sometimes ripe). Admittedly, the apples tended to have suspicious little holes and the citrus was on the puny side, which she insisted simply meant that no chemical, pesticide spray, or wax was used in their growth or handling. We also made our own yogurt, grew heirloom tomatoes in the greenhouse at our weekend retreat, and had meat shipped to us in New York City from a farm somewhere in Pennsylvania, where the cows were guaranteed—by whom, it wasn't quite clear—to have ingested only organic, hormone-free grains and grass.

Emily was not some hippy who wore patchouli oil and tie-dyed tops. No! At the time, she was an award-winning fashion designer, a founder and trustee of the renowned Fashion Institute of Technology, and best-selling author of beauty and grooming books. My father was the presiding justice of the New York State Supreme Court. Emily simply believed that "we were what we ate," and in order to achieve optimal health, we had to be extremely conscious of everything we put into our bodies.

Thanks to her, beauty and health became as much my passion as it had been hers. And at some point in my tenure at *Town & Country*, I took it one step further. I became involved with a cosmetic and fragrance industry initiative called "Look Good, Feel Better" that helped female cancer patients improve their appearance, and thereby self-image, by teaching them hands-on beauty techniques. From spending time with these courageous women, I also learned that they wanted, and needed, inspiration, hope, and the courage for living well beyond cancer to truly recover the *quality* of their lives. But many were so overwhelmed by their diagnoses, therapy protocols, and having to deal with all the psychological, physical, and social side effects that followed that they didn't know where—or how—to begin. I realized that in order for them to truly return to their normal—or better—quality of life, they had to understand that the traumatic effects of their illness went far beyond tumors and treatments. Therefore, the recovery had to help them overcome numerous lifestyle challenges, using diverse methods and modalities to assist them in achieving their objectives.

The Birth of Better Than Before

Working with a life coach, who was a three-time stage IV survivor, and a noted oncologist, I created a series of complementary steps—what we called Lifestyle Disciplines. After much trial and error, we came to the conclusion that in order to have a fuller, healthier, happier, and more rewarding life, it took more than just eating leafy greens and thinking happy thoughts. What was required was a multifaceted approach that included doctors' advice, an improved attitude, proper nutrition, easy exercises, renewed beauty and self-esteem, natural healing, a heightened imagination, a connection to a higher power, and a way to give back to the world to make it a better place. The survivor member of our team contended that these were essential in his personal recovery. The next part was putting these concepts in a format that would be easy for survivors to access, understand, and execute by themselves. They didn't need to be inundated with more complicated material or burdensome tasks.

Thus the Better Than Before program was born. Based on those early ideas for cancer survivors, I developed the concept, which features the *Ladder to a Better Quality of Life*, for everyone seeking to improve their lives. We all need coping mechanisms to help us face our day-to-day challenges. Perhaps the challenges are not a serious sickness or life-altering event, but simply mild depression and anxiety, or the desire to lose those last (or first) 10 pounds. At some point, we must all conquer lifestyle issues, large and small, that keep us from achieving the quality of life we most desire, but oftentimes we have resigned ourselves to consider it impossible to attain.

Begin the Climb

A simple visualization technique, the ladder, is an easy and effective tool. Each rung initiates an important lifestyle change to help you conquer the quality-of-life concerns that confront us daily, while offering advice to help you relax, renew, and replenish. Once you are comfortable with each rung, you can, and should, add what works best for you and subtract those that do not, taking into account your own feelings, along with the advice and recommendations of your family, friends, physicians, and caregivers. At the end of each chapter are worksheets for your notes.

My purpose in writing this book is to guide you over any obstacles and ease you onto a smoother path. Your actions and experiences make you who and what you are, so your mistakes are as important as your successes. It is not necessary to strive for perfection. Failure is highly undervalued. Just as long as you continue to go in the right direction—and that is moving upward. As my mother used to say, "Hitch your wagon to a star." But don't expect to revamp your life overnight. Your aim should be to improve each day through incremental changes. Above all is the understanding that every one of us can use guidance and encouragement to find hope and a renewed sense of self, energy, and enthusiasm. The Ladder will give you the access and options to help get you there.

So join me in making the fortune teller right! Let's take this journey up the Ladder, you and I, visualizing ourselves ascending out of our physical or emotional angsts and up to a more satisfying quality of life. Together we will explore, dream, discover, and draw on our internal unicorns—and just a touch of glitter—as we climb to making each day, each minute, just a little Better Than Before.

Doctor's Orders

"The physician heals. Nature makes well."
—Aristotle

A Healthy Lifestyle Is the Best Medicine

I have devoted practically my whole life to holistic and homeopathic remedies, as well as healthy lifestyle approaches. Yet here I sit, with a stainless steel rod, a plate, and 10 screws in my lower-left leg, along with a brand new right hip. So I have also learned to have a healthy respect for the traditional and allopathic (symptom-based) work of the medical community. In fact, one of the points that I constantly emphasize is that traditional medicine offers a wealth of extremely important information and applications that simply cannot be ignored. And those who are open and willing to investigate nontraditional areas must do so knowing that medical research is the primary source of this knowledge.

After all, underlying all the advances that affect our health are the basic elements of biochemistry. Take trans fats, for example. That evil hydrogenation process that makes those little cream-filled cupcakes all the more hardy is the addition of hydrogen to the carbohydrate molecules. Like a stopper in a drain, it blocks the oxygen atoms in the air that lead to spoiling from getting in. Through "hydrogenation," though, the fats and oils become inert—and the shelf life of the little cream-filled cupcake extends into the next century.

But do you really want those same molecules floating around your digestive tract and bloodstream? (Hint: The answer is "No!") Commercial baked goods may not succumb to the ill effects of oxygen and sunlight, but your system won't be able to break them down as easily either. In other words, trans fats remain just as inert in your gut as they are on the grocery shelves. On the other hand, it is well established that high-fiber foods absorb fat and cholesterol as they travel down your digestive tract, reducing the amounts that the body absorbs. So, traditional biochemistry helps us understand the problem—and the alternative therapy of good nutrition helps solve it.

A Multifaceted Approach

Platitudes abound these days as everyone seems to be getting on the health-and-wellness bandwagon, but whom should we believe? And, why doesn't our healthcare system concern itself more with wellness than illness? That is a question I am often asked. Well, happily—and increasingly—today's medical practitioners are becoming more aware and supportive of the concept of integrative medicine, which combines traditional medicine with complementary therapies to treat the mind, body, and spirit, with a focus on prevention.

Indeed, when I first started developing the Better Than Before Ladder for cancer survivors, many were confused about what to do once their treatment protocol was completed. After I explained my multifaceted approach to Dr. Rodney Sherman, a renowned New York City oncologist, I was heartened when he agreed with the concepts and even offered to help further develop the program. "We in the medical profession, and particularly in oncology research and treatment, are justifiably proud of the enormous strides that have been made in both extending the lives of cancer patients and making their protocol less debilitating," he told me. "Our main goal is to provide patients with optimal cancer treatment while working with them to maintain a high standard for their quality of life.

As a result of these efforts, more and more patients diagnosed with cancer are living longer with a much greater potential for returning to a normal life."

> "It is not an easy task to help survivors get back the satisfying quality of life they desire. Doctors cannot do it alone, and too often patients cannot do it either—it must be a team effort. Once their treatments are completed, it is up to the survivors to take over. We know they need to make certain lifestyle changes in order to achieve their goal—improved attitude, proper nutrition, easy exercises, renewed beauty and self-esteem, alternative medicine, family support, a heightened imagination, a connection to a higher power, and an opportunity to give back to others."
>
> —Dr. Rodney Sherman, Oncologist

Dr. Sherman was convinced that once survivors started incorporating simple changes, such as a positive attitude, proper nutrition, and family support, into their daily routines, they could better appreciate their second chance at life and enjoy it even more than they did before—further evidence that I was on the right track!

My personal journey over the past few years has made me eternally—or shall I say, internally—grateful to the miracles of modern orthopedic medicine. As for my husband, The Lawyer, he has three invisible drug-eluded coronary stents that undoubtedly saved his life. (He claims genetics are at fault, although I'm convinced it was his premarital diet.)

Yet those who know me realize that structuring my career around working with doctors—for my columns, radio show, and now this book—was perhaps ill-advised. You see, I am a confirmed hypochondriac who lives by a disease-of-the-day book. (But there is no guarantee, alas, that today's disease—hives—won't ultimately require a heart transplant.) Actually, I like to refer to myself as a "health alarmist," although under either name it leads to the same emergency rooms. Every illness that a doctor (or a chance acquaintance) mentions to me, I either think I have or I start to immediately experience the symptoms. I am always certain that I have come down with something both life-threatening and trendy—like the *Andromeda Strain*. And every time I take a walk by a medical office, I am tempted to run in for a quick CT scan, cardiogram, or complete blood count—just to be sure.

However, my personal neuroses aside, I advise getting regular check-ups and preventive screenings, which can be life-saving. If you are currently suffering from symptoms, I strongly suggest your condition be appropriately diagnosed by medical experts and that you are on the appropriate protocol, if necessary.

Have Some Faith

Doctor's Orders is the first rung of your climb up the ladder because it is the starting point from which most of us base our personal efforts toward better health and well-being. Of course, the odds of a doctor's advice working for you often depend on your trust in him or her. Having faith in your physician will not only help you maintain a positive attitude, but you will also be more likely to follow the prescribed treatment. So, if you don't believe in your doctor, find another one!

In order for you to develop that comfort level with a physician, come to the visit prepared with a list of questions and engage him or her in a *two-way* conversation. If you read an article or have information related to your condition, bring it to his or her attention and ask if it is relevant to your care. If you are unable or uncomfortable speaking up, designate someone who will advocate for you. Or have a friend, relative, or caregiver go with you and speak on your behalf. Also, the person you bring to your appointment can help you remember and digest all of the information provided. The more you know, the more you will be prepared to make the right decisions. Trust your inner voice and then act on what it tells you; because even when you have confidence in your physician, you must still be your own health advocate.

In Control

What makes a person at risk for illness? Some factors, such as age, ethnicity, and family history, are out of our hands. However, experts believe that up to 80 percent of illnesses, such as heart disease and type 2 diabetes, can be prevented by lifestyle changes. In other words, while genetics may load the gun, lifestyle pulls the trigger.

Even if you are receiving treatment and taking medication for a condition, adding simple disciplines to your everyday regimen can help you achieve optimal health. Not only will healthy habits make your medication or other treatments work more effectively, they may reduce or eliminate the need for medication.

Ultimately, following doctor's orders *and* adopting healthy habits are the best prescription for wellness. We can find examples of how that "prescription" works in nearly every condition. While we can't possibly cover every ailment in this book, let's look at the top six maladies, starting with cancer, which is where I first began my professional odyssey so many years earlier.

When it comes to illness and longevity, there are some people who seem to defy the odds. Take, for instance, someone touted as the world's oldest person—she is a member of the Kaxinawá tribe, found in the Brazilian Amazon. At 120-years-old, she believes her longevity is due to her lifestyle. She eats no salt, sugar, or processed food, but sticks to Amazonian staples such as monkey, manioc, and banana porridge. (Try finding that mix at your local Trader Joe's!)

The Big C

Cancer is the diagnosis everyone fears, and there is no single remedy for survivors. However, Jackie's story has much in common with many of the survivors with whom I spoke.

"I noticed an unusual lump during a breast self-exam," she begins. "Although I knew something was different, I convinced myself it was nothing and pushed away any lingering fears. After all, there was no family history of breast cancer." Eventually, the nagging feeling that followed her as she went about her daily routine won out, and she called her physician who referred her for a mammogram. That decision, along with the care she received, probably saved her life.

Her doctor was concerned enough with the results to suggest a biopsy. Jackie, though, was aware of what can go wrong in medical settings. So she insisted on a DNA-matching test to confirm that the surgical biopsy samples being evaluated actually belonged to her and that there hadn't been any mislabeling or contamination. She was still shocked to learn that she had stage IIA breast cancer, but knowing that the DNA matched eased her worry that it might be someone else's result.

Jackie's medical team recommended immediate surgery followed by a chemotherapy protocol. It has been a few years since her diagnosis, and she is now cancer free. Still, to lower the risk of recurrence, she will continue to take medication for five years, which also serves as a daily reminder that she is a breast cancer survivor. Additionally, she started following a ketogenic diet (low carbs, no sugar) under the supervision of her doctor and has returned to the gym. Given this second chance, Jackie is determined to live as healthy a lifestyle as possible so that she can be even better than before.

Jackie hopes that others will learn that it is always best to take that extra step when it comes to your health. "Whether it's making an appointment with your doctor or requesting a test that prevents medical errors that can typically go unnoticed, you're worth it. And it could be a matter of life—or death."

To that end, I asked a group of leading specialists for their advice on how to start the process. Dr. Andrew Kenler, an assistant clinical professor of surgery at Yale Medical School who specializes in laparoscopic surgery and treatment of diseases of the breast, suggests: "Before you have a test or procedure done, understand what steps your doctor should be taking to prevent medical errors." When a patient comes into his office to get a biopsy taken, many are unaware that a standard biopsy process includes more than 20 steps, with multiple individuals in different locations handling the specimen. He explains that, at each step, human error can play a role, but a patient's own DNA can ensure this doesn't happen. "A Washington University study that was published in the *American Journal of Clinical Pathology* found that specimen contamination and mislabeling occurs in 3.5 percent of all biopsies."

Dr. Deanna J. Attai, the president-elect of the American Society of Breast Surgeons, who focuses her practice exclusively on the care of patients with benign and malignant breast conditions, recommends researching your diagnosis but making sure that you are conducting *directed* research. "Many patients make the mistake of looking up their disease online, but they don't really understand their specific condition, rendering much of the information irrelevant. Ask your physician to recommend reputable references, and be sure that you have enough information about your condition so that you spend your time reading articles most relevant to your unique situation."

The doctor also says to never be afraid to get a second opinion, even if it simply reinforces what your physician has already told you. Most physicians do not take it personally if a patient seeks one, especially when it involves a serious illness or major invasive procedure. Remember to get another opinion not only on the diagnosis, but also on the treatment plan.

We also owe it to ourselves to improve the success of any treatment by adopting healthy habits. There is an abundance of evidence to support the fact that proper nutrition, exercise, and relaxation techniques can help cancer patients both during and after treatments. (We'll talk more about these as we climb the Ladder.)

The Shape of Your Heart

People may not fear heart disease as much as cancer, but the prognosis is every bit as serious. It is, in fact, the number one cause of death due to illness in this country. And it affects men and women alike, although men generally develop heart disease up to 10 years earlier. For females, the onset often comes after menopause, in part due to the lack of estrogen, which has protective effects.

So when The Lawyer with the three coronary stents announced to the waiter, "I'll have the steak," I was understandably upset, even though he asked for a lean filet mignon. Judging by the look of self-satisfaction on his face, he was obviously proud of himself for not ordering what he really wanted—the marbled prime rib.

I couldn't resist responding, "While you're at it, dear, why don't you have cheesecake for dessert, just in case you have any arteries left unclogged."

I would be remiss not to mention that The Lawyer, dietary deviations aside, is in very good shape for a man his age and is extremely aware of what constitutes a healthy lifestyle. (Thanks to me, naturally.) But that doesn't always mean he makes the wisest menu choices when it comes to his heart. He, of course, swears that a genetic predisposition—and my constant nagging—are the primary culprits for his prior coronary clogs. Therefore, I frequently remind him (always in calm, constructive tones), that he is just plain wrong.

Dr. Gordon Tomaselli, former president of the American Heart Association (AHA) and chief of the Division of Cardiology at Johns Hopkins University, backs me up on this. One in three Americans has some sort of cardiovascular disease, which can include hypertension (high blood pressure), coronary artery disease, heart failure, or arrhythmias (irregular heartbeat). He attributes a new uptick in coronary crises to a sedentary lifestyle, obesity, diabetes, smoking, and diets rich in processed foods.

Dr. Tomaselli stresses that we must turn our attention from risky to healthy behavior. For a start, that would include what the AHA refers to as Life's Simple 7:

1. Get Active
2. Eat Better

3. Lose Weight
4. Stop Smoking (smoking damages your entire circulatory system and increases your risk for coronary heart disease, hardened arteries, aneurysm, and blood clots)
5. Control Cholesterol
6. Manage Blood Pressure (normal is less than 120 mm Hg systolic and less than 80 mm Hg diastolic or <120/80)
7. Reduce Blood Sugar

When it comes to getting active, there is a preponderance of evidence that shows exercise can strengthen your heart, lungs, and blood vessels. The AHA recommends 150 minutes of moderate-to-vigorous activity a week, which can be broken down into sessions of as little as 20 to 30 minutes of activity five or six days a week.

Eat better to lose weight, control cholesterol, manage blood pressure, and reduce blood sugar. Fat—especially if a lot of it is around your waist—puts you at higher risk for many health problems and is especially bad for your heart. According to the AHA, if your body mass index (BMI, a measure of body fat based on height and weight) is 25.0 or higher, you will benefit by bringing your number down below 25. If your BMI is 30.0 or higher, you are at significant risk for heart health problems.

"If a person has had a coronary event in the first place, then clearly life changes need to be made," says Dr. Suzanne Steinbaum, director of Women and Heart Disease at the Heart and Vascular Institute at Lenox Hill Hospital in New York City and a spokesperson for the American Heart Association. "Eighty percent of the time you can prevent a repeat performance by making healthy lifestyle choices. Start by incorporating fruit, vegetables, whole grains, legumes, beans, olive or canola oil, and fish into your diet, and getting rid of all the saturated fats and simple 'white' carbohydrates, such as rice, pasta, bagels, and potatoes. Know that exercise is the best medication, and don't forget to smile and breathe. Believe it or not, perspective is everything, and being pessimistic and hostile can be damaging to your heart. On the other hand, having a positive outlook and a glass-half-full approach can help your heart's vitality and spirit."

Studies presented at a recent AHA's Scientific Session confirmed that women who drank more than two sugar-sweetened drinks a day had increasing waist sizes but weren't necessarily gaining weight, reports Dr. Christina Shay, lead author of the study and assistant professor at the University of Oklahoma Health Sciences Center. "These women also developed high triglycerides, and women with normal blood glucose levels more frequently went from having a low risk to a high risk for developing diabetes over time." This put them at higher risk for a heart attack.

Lack of exercise and an unhealthy diet, along with smoking and genetics, are unquestionably the most important risk factors for heart disease. But stress is also a huge factor. So "it is critical to make the connection between your emotional health and the health of your heart," says Harvard assistant professor of psychiatry Dr. Paul Hammerness. "At its extreme, heart injuries and heart failure can occur during severe emotional stress. This is called stress cardiomyopathy, or 'broken-heart syndrome.' Less dramatic but far more common examples," he claims, "include the well-known impact of anxiety and depression on heart disease and recovery from heart disease." And as corroborated by a major and well-regarded Danish study, he notes that the relationship between mood/anxiety and heart disease appears to be a "dose-response relationship," meaning that greater sadness and anxiety lead to greater heart disease and/or worse heart outcomes.

Therefore, one key step in caring for your heart is caring for your emotional health and working diligently to reduce levels of stress in your life (see Rung 2). When all is said and done, a calm, organized life may actually save your life.

Of course, along with these lifestyle changes, it's important to have your blood pressure, cholesterol levels, and blood sugar tested regularly. If you already suffer from hypertension, high cholesterol, or elevated blood sugar, more frequent monitoring is required.

More saving.
More doing.℠

1625 SYCAMORE AVENUE
HERCULES, CA 94547 (510)245-9672

1044 00003 48146   02/29/16   12:09 PM
CASHIER F_ORTIZA - FVT6889

090489246228 23 OSB PNL <P>
  0.535IV X 23 OSB PNL <P>   4.35
  0.535IV X 47.7IN OSB
0000-999-735 CABIN X 47.7IN OSB
  CA LUMBER FEE FEE <A,U>   0.04N
7503014652027 WAXING <A>
  #3 WAX RINGKIT   5.74

                     SUBTOTAL   10.13
                     SALES TAX   0.91
                     TOTAL $11.04

XXXXXXXXXX 2   USDEBIT 11.04
                                        TA
                                      VISA

Bone Up on Your Bones

Arthritis

Less fatal, but considerably more common, is the pain and debilitation of arthritis. About 50 million Americans have been diagnosed with one of the seven common forms. Yes, I am one of them. But it would take another book to tell you the stories about my recent hip replacement!

"Arthritis is a complex family of musculoskeletal disorders consisting of more than 100 different diseases or conditions, divided into three major categories: osteoarthritis, rheumatoid arthritis, and juvenile arthritis," says Patience White, M.D., professor of medicine and pediatrics at the George Washington University School of Medicine and Health Sciences and vice president of public health for the Arthritis Foundation. "Although common belief is that arthritis is a condition affecting the elderly, two-thirds of people with arthritis are under the age of 65, including 300,000 children. Also, arthritis affects people of all ethnicities."

The vast majority of current sufferers, about 27 million Americans, have osteoarthritis (OA), which is characterized by a breakdown of joint cartilage. The rest of arthritis sufferers have the more severe form: rheumatoid arthritis. Per Dr. White, "rheumatoid arthritis (RA) is characterized by inflammation of the membranes lining the joint. Although it can strike at any age, women are typically diagnosed between the ages of 30 and 60, while male patients usually are older. There are about 1.5 million affected individuals in the United States. Finally, juvenile arthritis (JA) is a term used to describe many autoimmune and inflammatory conditions that can affect children ages 16 and younger."

The disease takes a heavy toll. "Each year, arthritis accounts for 44 million outpatient visits and more than 900,000 hospitalizations. In fact, it's the leading cause of disability in the United States and is a more frequent cause of activity limitations than heart disease, cancer, or diabetes. By some estimates, 67 million Americans will have arthritis by 2030."

So what can we do? Knee, shoulder, and, of course, hip replacements are the drastic remedies. And they are really the only full cures, since bone spurs and lost cartilage simply will not dissolve or regenerate in our present state of technology. Most arthritis sufferers, though, are not there yet. As even my orthopedic surgeon, Dr. Roy Davidovitch, director of the New York Hip Center, NYU Hospital for Joint Diseases will agree, it's only when your lifestyle is completely compromised and you can't take another moment of pain that you have to bite the bullet and get the joint replaced.

However, there is much to do in between. Says Phyllis Crockett, DPH, in the Express Scripts Rheumatoid Arthritis and Inflammatory Disease Therapeutic Resource Center, "Each patient is different, and a physician can help determine the best treatment plan, including managing the symptoms and pain of arthritis, starting with exercise. It is a valuable tool in the fight against arthritis. Osteoarthritis and RA patients particularly can benefit from both endurance and resistance training."

Maintaining a healthy weight and protecting against joint injury can help prevent OA. "Every pound of weight lost reduces the pressure on each knee by four pounds. Even a small weight loss can be a big help in fighting it."

For patients who are already on medication to treat the condition, adherence—taking medications as prescribed— is critical to healthier outcomes. But never self-medicate! "Combining over-the-counter medications with prescription medications can be risky and can cause side effects, such as an increase in gastrointestinal (GI) irritation or a GI bleed. And don't adjust doses or make changes to the medication regimen without checking with your healthcare team." Watch for drug interactions. "Some common drugs like acetaminophen can have an interaction with arthritis medications. Limit intake, and remember that acetaminophen often is a component in common sinus, cough/cold, and pain medications."

Diet can also play a role. Opt for an anti-inflammatory dietary regimen (see Rung 3—Nutrition) and go easy on acidic foods such as sugar, white flours, and alcohol. "Also, some foods and beverages can block the effects of arthritis medications," Crockett adds. "These include grapefruit, apple, and orange juice, as well as milk and yogurt. Wait at least four hours after taking medications before eating or drinking these. Exact times can vary depending on the disease and the treatment. Check with a trained clinician."

Arthritis, in its many forms, is a continuing challenge. But with continuing focus it is possible to manage it successfully.

Osteoporosis

While we are discussing bones, we need to talk about osteoporosis, literally porous bones. After you turn 50, it's a good idea to measure your height every year, which will assess your posture and skeletal health. A decrease in stature can be as informative as a change in a bone density test for monitoring your overall bone health.

If your doctor determines that you have osteoporosis—or osteopenia, a precursor to it—it's still no reason to stress. True, the diagnosis creates visions of shattered bones and rounded backs, but it may just mean that you have a higher risk for fractures. And in the past 15 years or so, doctors have learned a lot about how to prevent those breaks.

Says Ethel S. Siris, M.D., director of the Toni Stabile Osteoporosis Center of the Columbia University Medical Center at New York-Presbyterian Hospital, "We now know that bone density loss is tied to decreases in calcium and impacted by low levels of vitamin D. So just make sure you take enough calcium and vitamin D every day. I generally recommend 1,200 milligrams of calcium from food or supplements, and 1,000 to 2,000 international units (IU) of vitamin D." Your doctor may also prescribe a bisphosphonate drug to lower fracture risk.

But don't sit around in fear of breaking your bones, which can actually be counterproductive. Load-bearing exercise, such as walking, is good for all bones. An exercise routine can not only preserve bone mass, it can improve flexibility, strength, coordination, and balance—all of which can help a person avoid falls.

Don't overdo it, though. And if you are close to someone with osteoporosis, try to sensitively steer her or him into sensible habits. As Dr. Hammerness advises: "Be clear about what concerns you, and get the facts so that you can have a reasonable conversation. Emphasize that you want your loved one to keep enjoying her favorite activities—as long as she makes her health an equal priority. If she's a hiker, for example, propose that she go only in daylight, avoid areas known for unstable terrain, wear boots with good traction, carry a walking stick or trekking poles for balance, and take a hiking partner. Remind her that by minding her own safety, she can do what she loves for much longer."

While for the moment, arthritis and osteoporosis may be incurable, the symptoms can largely or wholly be managed or even prevented.

Breathe Easy

There is nothing we take more for granted than breathing. Until we can't! Many moons ago, working through weeks of intense negotiations in smoke-filled conference rooms, The Lawyer began to suffer from what he thought were allergies. He ended up in the hospital for eight days with pneumonia. Happily, antismoking rules and more powerful antibiotics lessen the incidences of that now. However, in its place, we have almost an epidemic of asthma and, whether you believe in global warming or not, seemingly the same for allergies, and the two can be related. So much so that 50 million Americans are affected by them, and the numbers are growing.

The first time I came face to face with asthma was when my daughter, Elise, was in ninth grade and I got an urgent call from the school nurse, who told me Lisi was having trouble breathing. I dropped everything and raced up to her school. When I arrived, her chest was tight and she was still coughing and wheezing—all classic symptoms of asthma. What possibly could have triggered this sudden attack?

The nurse had an answer: "It came on right after she ate a pear. Probably some chemical in the skin."

As we drove off to the pediatrician, I noticed the nurse running after the car, frantically flailing her arms, a half-eaten pear dangling by the stem in one hand. She caught up and tossed in the offending fruit. "Here, take this with you," insisted the nurse, no doubt a *CSI* devotee, "to be inspected."

The good news? My daughter wasn't poisoned. But we were faced with the diagnosis that she had childhood asthma. Fortunately, after a few years of needing an inhaler from time to time before she exercised, she eventually outgrew it. Nevertheless, to this day, she has never eaten another pear.

No one is certain what causes asthma—most scientists believe it is partly genetic, partly environmental—and while some children, like Elise, see symptoms resolve with age, there is no cure. It is known that inhaled allergens and irritants, such as smoke, pollen, dust, mold, and strong odors and fumes, as well as certain common products and foods, even a beloved furry pet, can cause the airways leading to the lungs to become inflamed and swollen. Furthermore, the difficulty in breathing experienced by asthmatics often leads to anxiety attacks. And when stress levels increase, so do asthma symptoms. It's a vicious cycle.

Living with chronic asthma is challenging. So the first thing to do is to approach it head-on. "Managing asthma is a team effort," advises Dr. Norman H. Edelman, the American Lung Association's (ALA) leading medical authority. "Patients (or parents) should work with their healthcare provider to develop an 'asthma action plan' such as the one developed by the ALA, specifying medications and how to alter them if the condition worsens. For children, the action plan should involve teachers and school officials."

It is important to know that asthma and allergy triggers can come from the unlikeliest of places. For example, our homes can carry five times more pollutants than stepping outside since we breathe the same air over and over again. And The Lawyer, who seems to be allergic to exercise classes, was thrilled to learn that triggers can also be found lurking in health clubs. Unfortunately, Richard Weber, M.D., former president of the American College of Allergy, Asthma, and Immunology Organization of America (ACAAI) confirmed his suspicions: "Not only can new workout routines be difficult for those with asthma or allergies," he said, "but yes, many allergens that cause coughing, sneezing, wheezing, or rashes and watery eyes can indeed be found in gyms."

So be wary of the following culprits:

- *The Pool*—If you are sensitive to chlorine and don't have access to a saltwater pool that naturally disinfects the water, be sure to shower immediately after swimming.
- *The Locker Room*—A study published in the *Journal of Environmental Health Perspectives* found a link between triclosan, a common ingredient in antibacterial soap, and allergies. Since these cleansers are found in practically every locker room, bring along your own unscented products.
- *The Mats* (yoga or exercise)—According to the ACAAI, most rubber mats contain allergy-inducing latex and other available options could be laced with toxic PVCs. If you have had allergic reactions to either of these, it's best to tote along your own mats made of hemp or organic cotton.
- *Workout Outfits*—The ACAAI recommends staying away from materials such as polyester and nylon, which can also be itch-inducing, especially anything that says it's "odor-free" or "antimicrobial." Better to look for natural fiber or naturally wicking wool.

Fortunately, allergies can usually be treated with over-the-counter antihistamines. If symptoms are more chronic, your doctor may prescribe medication to take on a regular basis or even desensitization shots. If you want to know what you are allergic to, you can see your local allergist and be tested.

Dr. Joan Lehach, an integrative medicine physician specializing in allergy, asthma, and clinical immunology at Montefiore

Medical Center in New York City, offers a few suggestions on how those with pollen allergies can breathe a bit easier during the high-pollen times:

- If you live in a suburban area, keep your grass short and have someone else mow it. If you are going to do yard duty, wear a well-fitting allergy mask.
- Do not hang your wash to dry outside, because pollen bonds to fabric.
- Pollen counts are the highest early in the morning, between 5 AM and 10 AM, so do outdoor activities such as jogging in the evening or after 10 AM
- Pollen tends to stick to hair, so wash your hair more frequently.
- Keep your car windows and your windows at home closed, and put the air conditioner on. Use the recirculate button on your air conditioner so you are not bringing pollen in from outside.
- Beware of fruit. Because the proteins are similar, your body can mistake fruit for pollen and create some mild local reactions. Those who are allergic to trees should avoid apples, peaches, and pears. If you are sensitive to grass, avoid melons, celery, and kiwis because they can trigger an itchy mouth and throat.

Following these suggestions, along with carrying your inhaler if need be, will allow you to breathe easier wherever you go.

Forget Me Not

When my three kids were 4, 10, and 14, I took them on one of our weekly massive food shopping expeditions. We dutifully reloaded our shopping cart with the customary slew of bags at the checkout counter. Then off we went to load our SUV, which was parked on the street because the supermarket lot was full.

After making sure that everyone was securely buckled in, we headed home.

As soon as we arrived, the boys jumped out and left me to tend to the bags in the back. (Typical!) However, *there were no bags.*

"Boys," I said in the calmest tone I could muster under the circumstances, addressing the two older offspring, "what happened to the shopping bags?"

They simply shrugged disinterestedly, but my little daughter, obviously feeling bad at how frazzled I was becoming, finally chirped, "I think we left them on the 'stweet.'" Great!

At the time, I chalked it up to my mind being overwhelmed, and therefore overstressed and forgetful. Of course, if anything like that happened today, I would fear more ominous implications. The older we get, the more we tend to worry about losing our minds—literally! And while I'm not yet at an age when statistically I should be concerned about either dementia or Alzheimer's disease, there is a family history. So every time I can't find my keys or I'm madly looking for my lost cell phone—only to discover that I happen to be talking on it at the time—I fear the worst.

"How do I know if I have Alzheimer's," I recently asked a leading Manhattan neurologist. "I tend to lose things, and it's beginning to upset me."

"Well," he explained, "everyone misplaces their keys, for example, every now and then. It's when you are actually holding them in your hand and you don't know what to do with them that you should begin to worry."

Alzheimer's disease (AD) is anticipated to be the largest health crisis of our lifetime. Already, it is the sixth leading cause of death in the United States and more than five million (one in eight) older Americans suffer from it. Happily, there is new scientific research and evidence that suggest patients may be able to delay or prevent the onset of AD with a careful diet. At the helm of this research are Harvard-trained neurologist Dr. Richard Isaacson and nutrition researcher Dr. Christopher Ochner. They contend that targeted nutrients and aggressive dietary changes could improve memory in AD patients and those with mild cognitive impairment (MCI). In fact, following a brain-healthy diet will benefit anyone who's over age 40, has a family history of AD, or is experiencing problems with memory.

The doctors believe that nutritional interventions can indeed buy time for AD patients and their families. And thankfully, scientists have found a predictive marker for AD, a protein called amyloid beta that can be detected up to 25 years before the onset of the disease. "This gives future AD patients time to implement neuroprotective measures," advises Dr. Isaacson. "And new research shows that specific nutritional interventions may delay the onset of AD in memory-compromised patients by two years—potentially long enough for a cure to be discovered—and improve memory function in AD and MCI (or pre-AD) patients, a win-win for the patient, family, and caregivers."

Here are the doctors' 10 memory-boosting dietary recommendations, based on the latest scientific research and their clinical experience treating patients with AD and MCI:

- *Portion Your Macronutrients*—Every day, aim for 25 percent of your total calories from fat (but less than 7 percent saturated, or "bad" fat); 30 percent to 45 percent from complex carbohydrates (fruits, vegetables, and whole foods that are low on the glycemic index); and 25 percent to 35 percent from high-quality lean protein.
- *Wean Yourself Off High-Glycemic Carbs*—These include sugars, high-fructose corn syrup, processed cereals and grains, ice cream, crackers, salty snacks, such as chips and pretzels, and anything made with refined white flour.
- *Have More Good Fat and Less Bad*—Brain foods high in good fats include olive oil, avocados, natural peanut butter, and certain fish. Foods high in bad or saturated fat include most fast foods, anything hydrogenated, dried coconut, butter, animal fats, milk chocolate, and cheese.
- *Boost Your Omega-3 Intake*—Omega-3 fatty acids (DHA and EPA) are essential for memory function and brain

health. Most of us don't get enough from dietary sources (such as fish), so consider high-quality pure fish oil supplements that contain a minimum of 250 mg of DHA in each capsule, and aim for 1,000 to 1,500 milligrams (mg) of DHA daily if approved by the treating physician.

- *Feed Your Brain Antioxidants*—Antioxidant-rich foods are great for mental function. Some of the best are berries, kale, 100 percent pure unsweetened cocoa powder, mushrooms, onions, beans, seeds, sardines, trout, and Alaskan wild salmon.
- *Consume Enough Brain Vitamins*—Ensure adequate intake of folic acid, B_6, B_{12}, and vitamin D in particular. If you're not eating vitamin-rich foods on a regular basis, it's good to supplement as needed in pill or liquid form.
- *Choose Whole Foods*—In general, whole foods have only one ingredient—for example, strawberries or broccoli. If you must have a convenience (manufactured) food on occasion, find those items with the fewest ingredients, especially ingredients that you readily recognize and understand.
- *Opt for Low-Fat or Non-Fat Dairy*—Any recipe you make can be just as good with non-fat versions.
- *Enjoy a Cup or Two of Coffee*—Caffeinated coffee, one to three cups early in the day, may be beneficial over time to your brain. Studies done in Europe over several years demonstrate that men who drank coffee regularly showed less of a decline on memory tests than those who did not drink coffee.
- *Fast 12 Hours at Night*—If you routinely wake up at 6 AM, try to eat your last meal at 6 PM the night before. There is scientific evidence that substances called ketone bodies, which are produced when there are no carbohydrates to burn for fuel, may have a protective effect on brain cells.

It is important to note that just like the muscles in your body benefiting from a workout, exercising your brain on a daily basis is critical for successful aging. In fact, research now suggests that regularly engaging in activities that stimulate the brain, such as doing crossword puzzles, playing chess, or reading, may help improve memory, enhance motor skills, and reduce the risk of getting dementia. Above all, stop worrying that you might have Alzheimer's! Stress takes its own toll. So relax! Just remember the next time you inadvertently place your iPhone on the roof of your car while you are fumbling for your keys and then drive off with it still there (who me?) that you can still have many memorable years ahead if you watch your diet and give your brain a regular workout.

Fighting Depression

Emotional well-being is the next rung on our ladder, but I wanted to talk about depression from a medical standpoint. Clinical depression is a serious, but treatable, illness that affects millions of people. In fact, one in eight U.S. workers has been diagnosed with depression, according to a recent Gallup poll. Many "look perfectly fine, yet are suffering tremendously on the inside," says Massachusetts General Hospital's Dr. David Mischoulon, also an associate professor of psychiatry at Harvard Medical School. "Even as more companies offer wellness programs to promote good health, depression continues to take a toll in the workplace."

Interestingly enough, depression doesn't always manifest as sadness. Indeed, some chronically depressed people may just feel empty and apathetic, losing their passion for life. Trouble sleeping, loss of interest in pleasurable activities, feelings of guilt or hopelessness, decreased energy, trouble concentrating, appetite changes, and even suicidal thoughts or attempts have all been reported. One in six people will develop major depression in his or her lifetime. Surprisingly, two out of three individuals with depression do not receive adequate treatment, but it's important to realize that help is available and you can get better.

Clinical depression is generally caused by a combination of genetic, biological, environmental, and psychological factors. Furthermore, people with depression are more likely to have other medical conditions such as heart disease or diabetes, and they are also less apt to follow therapy for those problems, adding to their disease burden.

If you suspect depression, it's important to be diagnosed by a physician and explore treatment options. If you and your doctor determine that taking an antidepressant is the best course of treatment, Callie Carter, a specialist pharmacist in the Express Scripts Neuroscience Therapeutic Resource Center, suggests a few important tips to keep in mind:

- There is usually a lag of two to three weeks before medications begin to relieve symptoms of depression. It may take up to six weeks to see the full benefit, so be patient.
- Discuss symptoms that have not improved with your doctor. A different dose or medication may be needed.
- Antidepressant medication generally should be taken for at least six to nine months after a first episode of depression. The duration may be longer for subsequent episodes. Talk with your healthcare provider about the length of treatment, since early discontinuation increases the risk of depression recurrence.
- When antidepressants are discontinued, they should be tapered over two to four weeks to minimize side effects associated with abrupt cessation of therapy.

Chronic depression may be a terrible disease to live with, but once you find the right therapy you will happily discover a life that is indeed better.

At the end of the day, it is important to follow your doctor's orders. But be sure to be your own doctor, as well. I am a strong believer that taking your health into your own hands is not only empowering—it's an essential part of your journey to improved wellness.

Key Concepts from
Rung 1—Doctor's Orders

Concept _____

Why It Interests Me _____

_____

_____

_____

_____

How could I apply it to my life? _____

_____

_____

_____

_____

Concept _____

Why It Interests Me _____

_____

_____

_____

_____

How could I apply it to my life? _____

_____

_____

_____

_____

Concepts to Share

Concept _____

_____

_____

_____

With Whom? _____

_____

_____

_____

Concept _____

_____

_____

_____

With Whom? _____

_____

_____

_____

Concept _____

_____

_____

_____

With Whom? _____

_____

_____

_____

Emotional Well-Being

"Emotional Well Being—it's a choice. And when you bring awareness to any aspect of your life, you will reap benefits, because awareness tells you how you are doing. It's an infallible kind of radar, if you turn it on. The most important thing is knowing what you want."

—Deepak Chopra, M.D.

Here's to Your (Emotional) Health

With Dr. Chopra's words in mind, whenever I give a lecture on how to be Better Than Before, at some point I survey the room of (mostly) women and ask them what they want most out of life. The answer is almost always a resounding "We want to be happy!" Not to have more money, not to have more bags and shoes—although those are things that might make some people (ahem!) happier—but to feel happiness itself. To that end, I am often posed two questions: "Is it really possible to become happier?" And, "Can I do it overnight?"

The response to the first is a resounding "Yes!" As for the second, there are no instant fixes. In order to overcome life's emotional challenges, you must first take responsibility for your own life. Above all, you have to understand that your emotional lifestyle has consequences on your physical health, as well as your mental well-being. In other words, if you feel better about how you live, you will live better!

As we discussed in Rung 1, there is a direct link between emotional health and heart health. In fact, researchers at the Barbra Streisand Women's Heart Center at the Cedars-Sinai

Heart Institute have found that emotional stressors may trigger changes that can cause such health issues as coronary artery dysfunction, headaches, digestive problems, insomnia, and even cancer.

Stress is both inevitable and ubiquitous in most of our lives; yet we seem at a loss for ways to modulate it for ourselves. We all have so many responsibilities that we rarely allow ourselves a moment to think, to experience—to dream. And unless we get a handle on our lives, emotional angst can have serious consequences. But, what can we realistically incorporate into our daily lives to help get us through the difficult days? This rung is devoted to finding those ways and means.

The Kaizen Secret

The whole concept of being Better Than Before implies change—and the best place to start is in your mindset. Granted, it's not possible to become the pure, innocent five-year-old you, who (hopefully) never experienced an emotional crisis. But you can constantly try to be better than a day ago, an hour ago, or even a minute ago. The secret is to take small steps, what the Japanese call *Kaizen* (from the ancient Chinese words meaning "change to make good or better"). It is all about making an effort to continually improve each day in very small increments. You can begin by gradually replacing the negative self-talk that keeps you from becoming the person you truly want to be.

You Are Not Alone

We all suffer from something, be it as simple as cuticle biting, jaw clenching, or smoking; to more complex issues such as chronic stress, fears, low self-esteem, neuroses, and phobias. In response to these universal complaints, everywhere you look there's something either written or broadcast about stress management. What not to eat, what not to drink, what not to think.

The fact that you know you shouldn't be stressed—and you are—can cause even more stress. Take The Lawyer, for example, and his Orwellian theory on ice cream: "Forcing myself to resist my natural urges to eat it will cause more harmful stress than the physical LDL damage of eating it. So therefore, it will be even worse for my arteries to *not* eat ice cream!"(Huh?)

Chances are you are one of the millions of people who are overwhelmed in every aspect of their lives—at work, at home, in relationships, financially, and even by the little yet annoying things such as traffic jams and people with too many food items in the express checkout line. Unfortunately, the stress epidemic sweeping our country is not only widespread; it's also on the rise. Perhaps that's because the sources of stress are also multiplying.

> Stress is epidemic. According to the American Psychological Association, 77 percent of Americans say that they "regularly experience physical symptoms," 73 percent have "experienced psychological symptoms," and 48 percent feel that "their stress has increased over the past five years."

Stress Comes in Many Forms

The major personal stressors are well-known: Illness, dating and marriage, breakup and divorce, and the death of a friend or loved one. Then we all have career and financial worries. And for the more emotionally fragile, almost any change from their normal pattern can set emotional anguish in motion. Additionally, there are environmental stressors, such as smog and noise pollution. In today's digital world, stress may also come from a constant bombardment of e-mails, texts, and voice messages that gives us the feeling of being on-call 24/7.

However, the most difficult stress to deal with may stem from within—low self-esteem. It is most often triggered by trying to live up to the expectations of others—or what we assume others think of us. There will always be those who are more beautiful, wealthier, or more successful. You are who you are.

And if you are doing the best that you can, there is no reason to feel "less than."

We must also address the fears that turn into phobias and anxiety, that horrific sense of being out of control. It can be associated with a specific issue, such as flying, public speaking, driving on freeways, or even visiting the doctor. (Being that I am a hypochondriac, the very sight of a white coat, even on a butcher, causes my blood pressure to soar to stroke levels.) Anxiety can also manifest in that general sense of dread that comes out of nowhere, sometimes for no particular reason, but frightens the heck out of you.

That brings us to perhaps the greatest source of stress of all—motherhood, the veritable mother lode of emotional stress. No matter how good a parent we may be, we all feel (undoubtedly correctly) that we have made mistakes along the way. We fear, for example, that our kids will always remember the time(s) we sent them to school when they felt sick to their stomach, believing that it was only because we had other things to do—and the school nurse promptly sent them back home (secretly, I feared, thinking I was an unfit mother).

While we all make sacrifices for our children, every mother feels guilty about something. If we work, we wish we stayed home. If we choose to stay home, even for the first year or so, we think we should be doing more important things with our lives than discussing the relative merits of Pampers versus Huggies.

Sometimes we erroneously assume that we have the best of both worlds. When Elise, my youngest, was born, I began to write a few days a week from my home office. Granted, it was nice to secretly wear sweats and bunny slippers when I was doing important phone interviews. But unfailingly, every time I made a call, the children began to loudly attack one another in one made-up game or another. I would sigh and assert to my sympathetic interviewee that an inconsiderate coworker had brought his or her disorderly kids into the office.

For all you new moms, I do have good news—it does get easier with each child, I swear. For example, when Alex was a newborn, I used to rush him to the pediatrician whenever his temperature reached 98.7. With Philip, four years later as a more experienced mom, it was only when it got over 100. By the time Elise came along six years after that, I wasn't even upset when her temperature hit 102. Knowing by then that a healthy child tends to fever high to naturally fight infection, I merely gave her a dose of liquid Tylenol and kept a close vigil. Suffice it to say, she's still alive and thriving.

Yes, dads suffer stress, too! But as women, we tend to have even more responsibilities. We are nurturers by nature; so, for the most part, child care is in a mother's domain. It's exhausting just thinking that it could be possible to have it all—if we do it all. And we can't. It's both physically and mentally impossible.

And trust me on this one, ladies, it is okay to not be Wonder Woman. She's the one who gets up at 5 AM, sprints to the gym, then showers, answers all e-mails, fixes her family a breakfast of flaxseed banana waffles with organic maple syrup, and is ready to go to the office as soon as she drives her 2.4 equally perfect children to school. Her male counterpart is just as accomplished. Not only does he hold down a high-powered day job, but he is a nationally ranked squash player and on weekends writes poetry when not competing in an Ironman Triathlon. In a pinch, he can reshingle his roof. But unless they actually hail from the planet Krypton, inside they're a hot mess!

And I know this in part from my brief foray into Super-parenthood. It was one winter, many moons ago; I had really felt sorry for my husband as he somehow managed to always get sick at the exact same time as the children. Needless to say, he did not get a whole lot of sympathy. So when everyone was well, I decided to make it up to him. "Tomorrow, dear," I announced, "I will prepare you a special breakfast, lay out your clothes, and drive you to work."

So I spent more time fussing over his meal than I did taking care of the children that morning. They had cold cereal; he had steel-cut oats with walnuts. I carefully chose his suit and tie, and even made sure that he wasn't wearing one brown shoe and one black, as sometimes happens when he dresses himself.

And as soon as I rushed my older sons off to the bus and took my little girl to nursery school, as promised, I hopped in the car and gave him door-to-door service to his office.

An hour later, all missions accomplished, I, über-wife, returned to my office and started to write my column with still plenty of time left to meet my deadline. I sat back in the chair and let out a large self-satisfied sigh, thinking to myself, "Who said you can't have it—and, most important, do it—all?" Just then the phone rang.

"Mrs. Michael," stated the voice on the other end, "this is Mrs. Butters at the nursery school."

"Oh, hello, Mrs. Butters," I chirped. "Did the class enjoy those organic oatmeal raisin cookies I sent in the other day for their recess snack?"

"Those were great." She paused, then continued. "But the reason I'm calling is that you seem to have sent your daughter to school today in her pajamas." Bam!

And the Answer Is ...

So no matter our will and good intentions, we can't eliminate every source of stress. When I first began my research on how to help others feel better than before on an emotional level, what really stuck with me was a conversation that I had with a very spiritual person, a shaman, in fact. I remember asking her the true meaning of life. She said she would consult the Guides and get back to me. Finally, she called.

As I anxiously awaited her response, she replied, "Well, here it is." She paused. "Stuff happens (okay, stuff was not the exact word she used). Move on!"

"Seriously? That's the answer to the meaning of life?" I asked incredulously.

"Yes," she insisted. "Don't dwell!"

Of course, that is far easier said than done. Ignoring the negative mental chatter that can bedevil us is tough. Setting positive goals is self-affirming, but it's how you handle the all-too-likely failure to accomplish them fully (or at all) that is the key.

The Journey

It's important to remember that it's the journey, not the final resting point, that matters in self-improvement—finding satisfaction in the tiny victories and incremental improvements along the way. That, in turn, will allow you to live in and enjoy the moment. Too often, we spend so much time worrying about the future that we don't appreciate what we accomplished that day, or even that minute. By never giving yourself credit for what you have achieved on a day-to-day basis, everything just jumbles together into one big "to-do" list. Life becomes the trip from hell instead of an enjoyable voyage. In the words of Ernest Hemingway: "It is good to have an end to journey toward; but it is the journey that matters in the end."

That is perhaps the real meaning of my shaman's cryptic message, "Never give up." All the genius in the world won't do any good without guts, tenacity, and passion. Estée Lauder once told me that when she was first starting out, if cosmetic buyers said no, she would wait outside their offices all day until they changed their minds. Vincent van Gogh sold only one painting during his lifetime; Elvis Presley got a C in music class; Winston Churchill at one point lost three elections in a row; Henry Ford's car manufacturing company went bankrupt—twice—before becoming the Ford Motor Company; Sigmund Freud was booed from the stage when he first presented his revolutionary ideas; and Albert Einstein was expelled from school for being a disruptive student. What would the world be like if any one of them simply gave up and didn't forge ahead?

"There is no single magic bullet for turning your life and your health around. It requires focusing on all areas of your life. Each component has a powerful effect on the whole system. And it goes beyond a health-promoting diet and lifestyle. It also requires being a guardian of your attitude and self-talk in order to program yourself to be more positive, adaptable, and committed to life. I do believe that there is a purpose to our lives, and taking care of our body, mind, and spirit is critical in achieving that purpose. So we need to be very good to ourselves and those around us."

—Dr. Michael T. Murray

How to Begin

As with all our rungs, we must start with general principles and then work down through specific ideas, techniques, and therapies. For overall emotional well-being guidance, my favorite stress adviser is personal empowerment expert and author of the best-selling *The Synthesis Effect: Your Direct Path to Personal Power and Transformation*, Dr. John McGrail.

"Emotional well-being is the central desire (and the right) of every human being, first and foremost, to feel safe, loved, validated, and in control of his/her life," he asserts. "Ironically we are all born that way, in perfect love and energetic harmony, and filled with perfectly formed and vastly abundant self-esteem and emotional well-being. Then life happens and we, at least most of us in modern Western society, get it beaten out of us, at least figuratively."

Here, per Dr. McGrail, are some common steps anyone can take to reclaim that wonderful childhood state of mind:

1. First, you must acknowledge that you are naturally resistant to change, even when you want it and know it will be a good thing. It is literally in our DNA to cling to the familiar, a condition called *homeostasis,* from the Latin words meaning the "same state." It is homeostasis, the emotional equivalent of inertia in the physical world, that holds us back and keeps us stuck.
2. Accept that you are going to feel somewhat uncomfortable during the process of changing your life and consciously decide to allow yourself to feel that way. It won't

kill you, and once you cross that emotional bridge, half the battle is over and you are in the process of learning what you need to know to be the new you.

3. Accept that all change—in fact, life itself—is always a process. Modern technology-driven society is becoming too used to expecting instant results and gratification; when you accept the concept of process, it can help you hasten the happy results.

4. Commit to being "at cause" with your life—most of us live in a state of being "at effect," that is, feeling as if life is happening to us and we are the victims of circumstances beyond our control. Being "at cause" is a fundamental shift in that thinking. It goes something like this: It is no one else's job to make me happy or safe or loved or confident or financially solvent or healthy, or anything. It is my job alone. Thus, my results will depend on my choices, what I do, think, say, and feel.

5. Choosing to live "at cause" also leads us to another huge requirement—it must come from within. Most of us think that if we just get the stuff we want—our money, career, love and relationships, whatever we think is missing—that all will be well. But it is only when we rediscover our internal balance that we can begin to enjoy what we have.

6. In order to establish true emotional well-being, we must balance and integrate all our energy streams—physical, emotional, and spiritual. And we must acknowledge that we are indeed spiritual beings, something much easier to do with all the new science that is providing the empirical evidence we Westerners require. As such, we are seeing major changes in virtually all our health and wellness disciplines.

7. Finally, to really feel emotionally sound and whole, pay as much attention as possible to making choices that serve the greater good, to be of service to others. It can be as simple as validating other people on a regular basis—say thank you to anyone who provides you with a

service. Say hello and smile at someone you pass on the street. As you watch him/her light up just from being acknowledged and validated, you will too.

The Specifics

We have now started on our journey—more aptly, our climb up the Ladder—toward being emotionally Better Than Before. Since there is no one solution for all of our slings and arrows of outrageous fortune, let's take on some of the most common stressors and consider the experts' best advice for tackling them.

Let Them Be Right

Sometimes, no matter how hard we are actually willing to work, we are often held back from achieving greatness by letting our own personal annoyances get in the way. These can create roadblocks that compromise the goals that we set out to conquer. And one of these self-induced petty dramas is trying to change others.

To get to the bottom of why we are, at times, our own worst enemies, I again sought the advice of Dr. John McGrail. He says that one of the most powerful and effective techniques is what he calls the "Art of Allowance." This is a very simple strategy that allows other people to be whom and what they are.

Dr. McGrail says that when we allow others to be themselves without trying to change them, we don't have to feel any negative energy. They then cease to have any effect on us, and we can go about living our lives the way we want to, and they can do the same. The plus is that we can use that recouped energy for ourselves.

The next step is to simply let others be right, a technique he first learned from *Don't Sweat the Small Stuff ... and It's All Small Stuff,* by the late Dr. Richard Carlson. According to Dr. McGrail, Dr. Carlson's premise was simple: There are many people out there who just have to be right to feel okay about themselves, so why not just let them? You see, when we let them be right—even when we know they are dead wrong—we give them the gift of feeling good about themselves; and this, in turn, makes us feel good about ourselves.

Don't Panic

I am by nature an anxious person. My beloved husband is exactly the opposite. And whenever I feel particularly on edge, he always reminds me to calm down. "Think of yourself as being a pebble in a stream" is one of his favorite sayings for these occasions. "And just let the turbulent water wash over you." I swear he should be teaching spiritual healing in an ashram instead of practicing law.

But am I the only Nervous Nellie who thinks she is just one unfortunate incident away from losing it all? Who has unfounded fears that at the first sign of forgetfulness, her loved ones will send her off to a home for the criminally bewildered? I know a host of folk who have chronic anxiety at some level—people who feel repeatedly stressed, overwhelmed, fearful, and even phobic, often accompanied by that awful, unsettled feeling in the pit of your stomach or a tightness in the chest that causes an imminent fear of cardiac arrest in the middle of the crosswalk.

Full-blown anxiety/panic attacks are not uncommon, either, and can sometimes appear to occur for no apparent reason. And therein is the basis for a vicious cycle. The fear of having an anxiety attack in a crowded elevator, or even such a nonthreatening place as, say, the dairy aisle of the supermarket, can actually trigger one. There is no question that chronic anxiety is a horrible condition—and the result is that you feel out of control in one, many, or even every aspect of your life. I know. I've been there.

Of course, the first place to start in fighting chronic anxiety is also the most difficult. Since it is almost always both irrational and psychosomatic (a physical condition caused by the mind), most, and usually all, of the fears and phobic reactions associated with it—dread, panic, physical weakness—are completely disproportionate to the actual risk involved, which is often little or none.

Thankfully, a situation irrationally created by the mind can be controlled by reinstating rational thoughts. Sure, we all occasionally entertain irrational thoughts that automatically pop into our heads but that we never act upon; for example, the thought of surreptitiously sticking out your foot and "accidentally" tripping an obnoxious coworker. (Admit it, you've also been tempted to do that.) We think of these things, and then we immediately exert cognitive, rational control and don't act; in other words, our morals and ethics—and natural sense of self-preservation—jump in to restore rationality and control.

The same procedure can be used to combat anxiety—which is, in effect, our irrational fear of losing control of our own lives. Of course, neither I nor anyone else can guarantee that you will be able to completely conquer your anxieties and phobias. Trained professionals like Dr. McGrail help many sufferers and are needed to help many more. But for many of us, anxiety can be overcome on our own, without a lot of medications. It's *your* mind, after all. You own it, you control it, and you can learn to drive it where you want it to go. However, if you do need help, do yourself a favor and get it!

Here are Dr. McGrail's specific recommendations on how to overcome panic attacks and chronic anxiety:

- *Stop the Mind—Ask yourself one of these questions, then wait: Where did I come from? What is nothing? What is thought? When you ask yourself a question with no immediate answer, your mind must stop. When it does, you cannot feel any negative feelings. You are once again back in control.*
- *Squeeze the Trigger and Breathe—Hold the thumb and forefinger of either hand together, gently but firmly. Focus all your attention on your fingers squeezing together; look at them, feel them, and then say to yourself (silently or aloud), Stop! Now begin to breathe, slowly and deeply, focusing on the air entering and leav-*

ing your body. You should calm down in a very short time. When you do, release the trigger.

- **Slow Down and Focus**—*That feeling of being overwhelmed is often caused by looking at situations in their entirety. It's like standing at the bottom of a tall, steep mountain and trying to imagine climbing it all at once. It's easily overwhelming. But if you just start walking one step at a time and only focus on the next step—with an occasional glance at the whole mountain so you stay oriented—pretty soon you're at the top looking down. The same can be said for the situations we deal with in life. We can slow down and commit to taking it one step, one choice, one thought at a time.*
- **Remember TAO**—*In this case, TAO does not refer to the ancient Chinese philosophy, but instead refers to the notion that **T**here **A**re **A**lways **O**ptions. For example, if you were stuck in traffic and absolutely had to leave the car, you could just get out and walk away. Sure it might cause others to call you names, but if it were necessary—life and death, say—the choice is there. So whenever you feel particularly anxious, just think TAO!*

Exercise to Relax

Besides using mental and psychological techniques to help combat anxiety and panic attacks, the time-honored blowing off of steam from a punching bag to a 5K run is still a very valid option! So I turned to Mark McGee, a 6th Degree Black Belt, senior instructor, t'ai chi and Qigong, for a physical exercise to help control emotional challenges.

According to Mark, Qigong is an ancient Chinese exercise that improves emotional well-being as it harmonizes the mind, body, and breath. Since anxiety is a root of many health problems, one of the best antidotes is to breathe deeply from a strong foundation. He recommends the following simple exercise for beginners, a more physical manifestation of Dr. McGrail's trigger squeezing.

Stand with your feet about shoulder-width apart. Take in a deep breath while raising your shoulders as high as you can comfortably, then let out your breath slowly while lowering your shoulders, hollowing your chest, rounding your back, lowering your chin, bending your knees slightly, and tucking your sacrum. Once you feel that you are close to being out of breath, inhale again and repeat the raising of your shoulders, followed by a slow exhale and full body relax. Use your mind during the exercise to focus on how good you feel as you nourish every cell in your body with the rush of air and natural stretching. And spend a minute afterward enjoying slow, deep breaths before returning to your work or routine.

Don't Worry, Be Happy ... But, It's a Process

Countering stress, anxiety, and phobias is critical to emotional well-being. But that only gets you halfway there. Being better than before not only means moving out of negative emotions but also into positive ones. So now we turn to how you can be positively happy!

Back to Dr. McGrail who is a big believer in the importance of finding your way to that positive space: "Happiness is a state of mind that you can choose any time you wish, even while you're in the process of resolving your issues and creating your better life. In fact, it will happen much faster that way." He says the two key points to that statement are *choice* and *process*.

With that in mind, Todd Patkin, who is as happy as The Lawyer is sensible, and the author of *Finding Happiness: One Man's Quest to Beat Depression and Anxiety and—Finally—Let the Sunshine In*, has a great plan for happiness.

Patkin says that society tells us (not very subtly, either) that we need to perform to a certain standard, look a certain way, weigh a certain number, make a certain amount of money, and much more. "Too bad that 'perfect' lifestyle is impossible to achieve. Nobody can do it all, all of the time. So when you inevitably take on too much and allow one of the plates you're juggling to drop, you end up disappointed, tired, and miserable."

According to Patkin, if you really want to experience true happiness and fulfillment, stop setting yourself up for disappointment by having unrealistic and unsustainable expectations. For the sake of happiness, here are his suggestions:

- *Give Up on Relationships*—The ones that aren't working, that is. You need to be around other people who share your commitment to happiness.
- *Stop Being So Darn Nice*—And start being real. Dishonest politeness doesn't develop authentic relationships. Having a smaller number of true friends is healthier than denying your own happiness in order to make everyone else like you.
- *Stop Working So Hard*—Everyone has physical and mental limits. And achievement doesn't equal happiness. Overloading on work will cause your relationships, mind-set, and even health to suffer. Really think about what a healthy balance looks like.
- *Lower the Bar*—You probably expect too much from yourself. Consciously lower your expectations to more realistic standards, celebrate your many successes, and stop beating yourself up.
- *Ignore the Joneses*—Keeping up with the Joneses seems to be the American way of life. But you need to understand the fundamental truth that "happy" for you won't look the same as it does for anyone else—and that's okay! Focus primarily on your own feelings and fulfillment.
- *Don't Focus on Your Spouse*—To the point where you forget to take responsibility for yourself, that is! Putting yourself second all of the time can breed frustration and resentment. Remember that when you do things that make you happy, it's good for your husband or wife, too.
- *Stop Giving So Much*—If you don't, you'll eventually run dry! Figure out what is important to you and what fulfills you.
- *Stop Pushing Your Kids So Hard*—Too much pressure to perform can cause children of any age to burn out and make self-destructive decisions. Your kids will be much happier, healthier, more creative, and more motivated

throughout their lives if you prioritize balance and love them for who they are.

- *Forget Quality Time with Your Kids*—And start focusing on quantity! Life is found in the everyday moments, not in the big blowout trips. Doing "normal" things with your kids on a regular basis will mean more to them— and to you—long-term than the occasional extraordinary event.

- *Cancel Your Gym Membership*—The key to instilling any habit in your life is to make it doable. So if exercise isn't already a regular part of your life, start small. Take a 20-minute walk every other day around your neighborhood—that's it! You can work up from there if you want to. And remember that exercise isn't just about losing weight; it's a natural antidepressant that will improve your sleep and make you feel more relaxed, stronger, and more capable of handling life's challenges.

- *Stop Obsessing About Your Health*—Just eat right, go to the doctor, and fit in as much exercise and relaxation as you can. If you don't, all the worry and stress will be what ends up killing you!

- *Trash Your Goals*—Except for this one—Be happier! When you prioritize your own happiness and well-being, you'll be truly amazed by how smoothly everything else falls into place!

It's 4 AM, you can't sleep, and you're obsessing over work, money, relationships, or your endless "to-do" list. Judith Orloff, M.D., a board-certified psychiatrist and assistant professor of psychiatry at UCLA and author of *The Ecstasy of Surrender: 12 Surprising Ways Letting Go Can Empower Your Life*, often gets that complaint from patients. In response, she offers some recommendations for alleviating common forms of stress:

- In a recent survey by the American Psychological Association (APA), money (71 percent), work (69 percent), and the economy (59 percent) were the most commonly reported sources of stress. To let go of this so-called "success stress," stop comparing yourself with others and focus instead on what you're grateful for. If you find yourself envying someone's success, ask yourself what you admire and can learn from them. Finally, wish them well. These simple strategies will help you change the way you think of success and will free you up to change some of your behaviors around money and work.

- Nearly half (46 percent) of adults in the survey said that within the last month they had lost patience with or yelled at their spouse, partner, or children when stressed. You can let go of relationship stress by staying calm, no matter what buttons your loved one has pushed. Avoid reacting or getting defensive. Let the other person completely finish talking, and then pause before you respond. Instead of trying to change someone's mind, accept where he or she is coming from and try to be compassionate. When we stop trying to control relationships, they become less stressful.

- In the APA survey, 30 percent of adults reported that stress had a strong or very strong impact on their physical health. Stress makes us tense, obsessive, and burned out by the hormones adrenaline and cortisol. Consequently, we become malnourished or overweight. We don't exercise, and the quality of our sleep suffers. One of the best ways to let go of physical stress is to let your body do what it was designed to do—move. Practice some kind of movement you like at least a few times a week, whether it's going to the gym, walking your dog, or doing yoga stretches. The goal of movement is to get out of your head and surrender to the body's natural energy.

For Cancer Survivors

As I was developing the Better Than Before program, many cancer survivors shared with me their psychological social stigmas. Some rejected any kind of personal interaction, or they seemed comfortable only when alone or around others who were willing to listen to their incessant talk about the horrors they have been through. Others had the opposite social struggles. They confessed that they wanted to strangle the next person who looked at them with either pity or what they termed "airplane" eyes, which always seemed to land directly on that spot. A few felt their friends purposely avoided them because they were afraid they might "catch it," even though it's not contagious. Most had difficulty dealing with the irritatingly positive people who constantly commented, "You can do it" or "You'll be just fine," without knowing a thing about what they went through. The most tactless ones, undoubtedly innocent in their intent, told them about all the people they knew who had the same type of cancer and how long they survived after being diagnosed.

After talking with many cancer survivors and patients, and many of their oncologists and therapists, I always try to pass on the following advice:

- *Deal with Your Demons*—Know that CDs—or cancer demons—those evil little voices that play over and over again in your mind telling you that you will most surely have a recurrence will never completely go away. Therefore you must learn to tame them. Accept that they are there, recognize that their mission is to make you miserable, marginalize them, and then converse with them.
- *Let It Be*—There is no way to control what other people say to you, but you can control how their statements affect you.
- *Don't Immerse Yourself in Guilt*—For example, "Did I cause my own cancer because of my negative personality? Or what did I—or didn't I—do in my life?" There is absolutely no research that says thinking negatively has anything to do with getting cancer. Or that you—or anybody else in your life—caused you to get it, either.
- *Let the Guilt Go Even More*—Don't feel bad if you're not positive 24 hours a day. Nobody can be. That's just putting too much pressure on you.
- *Get a Handle on It*—Dr. R. Duncan Wallace, psychiatrist and psychotherapist and author of *The Book of Psychological Truths*, says that "the cause of mental pressure is thinking illogically about the future in absolutes, such as

'I must have a good result,' or 'I can't let the illness get me'—trying to force future certainty. Instead, replace that with, 'I'll take whatever happens in the best way.'" This recognizes the true uncertainty about any outcome and immediately takes the pressure off your mind.

- *Create a Clear Picture*—Picture a healthy you in that vision. Be as detailed as possible, using all five senses—see it, smell it, taste it, touch it, hear it, and, finally, add a large measure of positive emotion.

- *Be in the Know*—Be aware that your thoughts have the power to create reality. In other words, how you think controls how you feel. Try to reframe your life by not letting your cancer define it. It is not who you are. Whenever you start to feel anxious, see yourself as strong, healthy, and vibrant, with the inner strength to overcome anything.

- *Use Visualization*—Our Ladder is all about using visualization on your climb. For survivors in particular, picture your body healing with great ease. Use your imagination to come up with what feels like the most pleasant image of healing—a golden light, a baby's hand, cleansing ocean waves—and smile as you actually feel yourself healing and remaining healthy.

Wrapping It Up

We've covered a lot of tips and techniques for improving emotional well-being. Remember not to take on too much all at once. Consistent, steady improvements are what count. In wrapping up, the following is my personal advice for emotional well-being, culled from years of working with patients, therapists, other experts, and, of course, some trial and error. Just pick the ones that are easiest for you to follow.

- *Clear Your Mind*—To clear and calm your mind of any anxieties, it is helpful to focus on your breath. For this exercise, you are going to breathe in to the count of six, then hold your breath full to the same count, breathe out to the count of six again, and then hold your breath empty to the same count. This goes in four sections: In, hold, out, hold. As you begin, you will find yourself counting a little too quickly, and then gradually, you will slow down your count and deepen your breathing. Doing this for just five minutes a few times a day will make a big difference in your ability to remain calm and steady. If you would rather talk than count, you can also say—I am going to be Better Than Before.

- *Be in the Moment*—This exercise involves mindfulness, the Eastern philosophical and spiritual practice that involves centering on the moment. Find a quiet place in your house. This time, imagine what makes you feel the most calm and relaxed. For example, visualize yourself lying by the ocean and listening to the waves or watching a magnificent sunset.
- *Beautify Your Surroundings*—Surround yourself with what you love and what gives you a warm feeling, whether it is family, friends, pets, or even keepsakes.
- *Get Over It*—Studies show that anger and bitterness put the body into a stressful state. Learn to have a loving and forgiving spirit. Feeling Better Than Before means learning to relax and enjoy life.
- *Laugh It Off*—Laughter heals. Laugh often, even until your sides ache. It is difficult to laugh and be depressed at the same time.
- *Take a Short Nap*—No more than an hour, once a day. Make sure you get at least seven hours of sleep a night.
- *Cut Down All Your Activity*—An hour before you go to sleep. That includes Internet, exercise, and TV. (If you have a favorite late-night program, tape it.) And dim the lights. Research suggests that this mimics sunset, and your brain responds by releasing melatonin, the hormone that brings about sleep.
- *Get Focused*—Prepare for the next day a "focused visualization" by writing a paragraph in as much detail as

possible on how to feel Better Than Before. Reading this aloud and planting the vision in your mind before bedtime allows your subconscious to work on your goals and dreams all night.

- *Write It Down*—If you still can't fall asleep after 20 minutes, get up and do something quiet, like reading a book—or work on that paragraph about how you want to feel the next day. Keep a pad by the bed and jot down any thoughts that might have slipped your mind earlier. You must let your body and mind slow down to ease into sleep. If you just lie there thinking about how you're not sleeping, all of your angsts are sure to pay you a visit.
- *Remember the "Horizontal Rule"*—No negative inner dialogue when you are horizontal (in bed). This is a time when the right brain (which represents creativity, imagination, intuition) tends to exaggerate the negative. So only focus on positive experiences and memories when horizontal.
- *Have a "Worry Hour"*—That is the time to problem-solve and do research, but, again, not in the middle of the night. It is best in the middle of the day when the sun is high, and your left brain (logic) is sharp.
- *Affirmative Action*—Make a list of inspiring quotes and affirmations that you have found and refer to them daily by putting them on your computer screen, bathroom mirror, fridge, or anywhere else you will see them. A favorite of mine is: "Every minute of every day I am becoming Better Than Before."

Mother Knew Best

I would be remiss not to give credit in this rung to the one person who most inspired me personally—my mother, Emily. She was an acclaimed author, syndicated beauty columnist, Coty Award–winning fashion designer, and a founder, director, and trustee of the prestigious Fashion Institute of Technology in New York City.

Sadly, Alzheimer's was the way her life ended. But she will never be forgotten. The heavens continue to shine brighter from her light. And not only did she leave behind a legacy of beauty, talent, and intelligence, her important work, notably as the first creator of clothes designed expressly for teenage girls—the inventor of Junior Miss—will live on forever.

There is one story in particular that I wish to highlight in this rung. I discovered it a while back when I opened a folder in my office and a paper fell to the floor. Although it may have been penned many years ago, it is advice that transcends the ages and holds true to this very day. And it even became the cornerstone of my philosophy.

It was entitled "People Aren't Born Happy … They Have to Work at It." Emily noted that happiness and beauty—not necessarily physical beauty, but the glow from inner peace that is considered universally beautiful—go hand in hand. Bitterness, hostility, anger, and depression are the enemies of loveliness, while laughter, joy, and peace are beauty's best friends. My mother noted that it would be wonderful if we could simply push a happiness button, but that's not reality. She said that if a cheery disposition doesn't come easily to you, conscientiously practice the art, just as you would a musical instrument. She claimed that happiness is making the most of every second and wondered why anyone would waste time on meaningless quarrels and malicious gossip. Life, she insisted, is way too short for negative or petty dramas. Much of what we worry about never happens anyway. And many of the other situations are totally out of our control as well. But nevertheless, we tend to allow minor irritations to morph into major issues in our mind. Worry, she maintained, is basically wasted energy and emotion.

She advocated enjoying life now and suggested that happiness is having a goal and objective, and contentment comes from ultimately realizing it. She stated that true bliss is the end result of believing in you, despite what others say or do. Happiness is learning to laugh about situations, even when the joke is on you. According to my mother, people respond positively to a happy personality. In her view, happiness is also reliving pleasant memories through reviewing old photographs, rereading a favorite book, or contacting a friend whom you haven't seen for years and laughing over old times. (This was way before Facebook and Twitter, mind you.) Finally, happiness is enjoying the little pleasures in life—the first snowstorm, a log fire, a delicious meal. She believed that you can't start a malady in a happy body.

As I mentioned, there is some advice that stands the test of time.

Key Concepts from
Rung 2—Emotional Well-Being

Concept _____

Why It Interests Me _____

_____

_____

_____

_____

How could I apply it to my life? _____

_____

_____

_____

_____

Concept _____

Why It Interests Me _____

_____

_____

_____

_____

How could I apply it to my life? _____

_____

_____

_____

_____

Concepts to Share

Concept _____

_____

_____

_____

With Whom? _____

_____

_____

_____

Concept _____

_____

_____

_____

With Whom? _____

_____

_____

_____

Concept _____

_____

_____

_____

With Whom? _____

_____

_____

_____

Nutrition

"Tell me what you eat and I will tell you what you are."
—Anthelme Brillat-Savarin

Food for Life

It wasn't that long ago that the only diseases associated with what we ate were gout and indigestion. Today, the connection between diet and a host of major and minor ailments and illnesses is both universally accepted and much better understood. In fact, our supermarket aisles have become our lifestyle pharmacies. Whether it's gluten-frees, omega-3s, mega-Cs, vitamin Ds, antioxidants, or probiotics, there is a plethora of products that have now entered the mainstream.

Back then, I also wrote my first book, *Breakfast, Lunch and Dinner of Champions*, in which I interviewed athletes in 10 major sports and discussed their nutritional needs and ideal regimens. Even then, a growing number of star players were becoming aware of how proper nutrition was directly tied to stamina, speed, consistency, and power.

Through writing about the athletes' dietary regimens, I learned of the high- or low-glycemic index theory. Our bodies quickly convert foods with a high glycemic index (GI), such as white bread, commercially baked products, sugary drinks, and alcohol, into blood sugar. That means a rush of energy—until, that is, our natural insulin kicks in to cleanse the excess from the blood. Then, all of a sudden, there comes a feeling of weakness, exhaustion, and lethargy, something a professional athlete would never want to experience.

Therefore, many athletes opted for what passed *then* as an enlightened complex carbohydrate diet based on the three *Ps*—pasta, potatoes, and pancakes. They found that choosing these types of foods two to four hours before the game gave them the sustained energy they needed to play, without having the highs and lows of simple carbohydrates (sugars). They also didn't want the fatigue from digesting heavy foods such as steak, which made more sense either long before—or after—the event.

Fast-forward to three decades later … although dramatic changes in the way we think about nutrition constantly emerge, the same basic precepts still apply. Food matters!

Granted, what we eat plays a much larger role than simply satisfying our hunger. Otherwise, nobody would grab for yet another slice of pepperoni pizza when they had already over-dosed on meatballs, and a jilted lover would not find solace in a box of chocolate-dipped cherries. We tend to eat out of loneliness, boredom, frustration, unhappiness, happiness, emotional emptiness, and also to reward ourselves for a job well done. It is the rare individual who celebrates a promotion with a huge workout on the elliptical machine.

Food is soothing; it never talks back (at least not right away) or criticizes, and it can always be there waiting for you when you come home from a stressful day. Sometimes, the joy of eating something sinfully rich can even replace sex in releasing feel-good endorphins (until the inevitable sugar crash a few hours later). In addition, a pint of chocolate-chip cookie crunch ice cream would never tell you that your behind "looks fat" in that dress. Of course, lurking beneath all the kindness and understanding is the sad truth: Eating too much ice cream is what undoubtedly gave you that fat behind.

The problem is there is such an oversaturation of information available about diet and nutrition that it's hard to know where to begin. So I am here to simplify. In a nutshell, carbohydrates and fats are our energy sources and proteins are what we are made of. Everything else that we eat only assists the body in processing and accessing these three (or does nothing or something insidious). Let's take a look at them one by one, and I'll give you a very brief lesson on how they work.

Carbohydrates

Of the three, this is the only one with an accurately descriptive name. Carbohydrate is the chemical term for molecules composed of carbon, hydrogen, and oxygen. They provide heat and energy. But when food experts and nutritionists speak about them, they are referring to the basic forms that appear naturally in our diets—sugars, starches, and fibers.

Sweet Talk

Pure sugar comes in six varieties. Glucose, otherwise known as dextrose or blood sugar, nourishes our bloodstream. Sucrose, which is by far the biggest source of sugar, is derived from sugarcane and sugar beets and is sold as white refined, brown, and confectioners' sugar, as well as other variants. Fructose, as the name suggests, is found naturally in fruit. However, far from natural, high-fructose corn syrup is an industrial food product that seems to be in everything these days, from processed foods and sodas to such seemingly innocent culprits as ketchup, breads, yogurt, salad dressings, cereals, crackers, children's vitamins, and Girl Scout cookies. Another clever marketing ploy is "evaporated cane juice." Sounds lofty and healthy; but it is simply sucrose refined from sugarcane in liquid form. Finally, there's lactose, or milk sugar, and maltose, the basic sugar in most cereals and grains.

The sad news is that Americans have increased their sugar consumption from minimal amounts to more than 160 pounds per person per year, according to the U.S. Department of Agriculture. Perhaps it isn't a coincidence that, along with this outrageous number, obesity rates and type 2 diabetes have multiplied as well. (I'm not saying it's the only reason, of course, but the statistics cannot be ignored.)

Sugar, as glucose and its more complex form, glycogen, is our fuel. In other words, it is pure energy. However, too much of it leads to insulin sweeps and possibly type 2 diabetes. How we process food into glucose involves the use of vitamins (notably the B vitamins) and enzymes. If what we eat doesn't contain these vitamins and enzymes, it actually leaches them out of our systems, creating nutritional deficiencies. Happily, nature tends to help us with that. Whole grains, unlike refined food, contain not only the source of the carbohydrates (usually as starch) but also the vitamins necessary to convert it into glucose.

Easy on the Starch

Simply stated, starches are a very complex form of carbohydrate, chemically akin to sugar. However, because of their structure, they are much more difficult for the body to process. Therefore, they don't rush right into your system; they burn much more slowly. This means that the blood sugar levels don't have to be stabilized by a sharp insulin blast from your pancreas into your bloodstream, which either converts the excess into fat or forces it out of the system entirely. However, not all starches are created equal. Products made with refined (white) flour, white potatoes, and white rice are more easily converted into glucose and cause spikes in blood sugar; while whole grains, fruits, and vegetables are examples of complex carbohydrates, which not only have more nutritional value and regulate blood sugar, but also provide fiber.

Go with the Flow

This brings us to all-important fiber, the missing link in refined and processed foods. Dietary fibers are the parts of plants that do not break down in our stomachs, instead passing undigested through our system. They are either soluble or insoluble, both types being equally important. *Soluble* fiber is found in such foods as flaxseeds, oatmeal, lentils, nuts, pears, blueberries, and oranges. The fiber attracts water and forms a gel that slows down digestion, therefore having the same healthy effect as eating food with lower glycemic index values—stabilizing our blood sugar levels—and making us feel full faster. Soluble fibers can also help lower the bad cholesterol (LDL) by interfering with the absorption of dietary cholesterol. *Insoluble* fibers don't dissolve in water and therefore pass relatively intact through the digestive tract, pushing through whatever may be in there in front of them. These are found in all whole grains, wheat bran, popcorn, dried fruit (especially prunes), and dark leafy greens. Insoluble fiber is the natural broom that aids in digestion and keeps our colons healthy.

Fats

Information about the kinds of fats we should eat and just how much seems to be constantly updated, leading to mass confusion. Before we get into that, know that fats have more than twice the energy potential per gram than carbohydrates. Even though they are also only composed of carbon, hydrogen, and oxygen atoms, they have a much more complex molecular structure. As a result, fat is slowly digested, leaving a longer feeling of satisfaction and providing sustained energy.

Spoiler alert! You would probably still be living in the Stone Age should you not be aware that the typical American diet is filled with all the wrong kinds of fats. But here's what you need to know in order to help you distinguish the good fats from the coronary artery cloggers. At the heart of fat structures are three types of molecules known as saturated, monounsaturated, and polyunsaturated fatty acids. The difference (and names) are based on the extent to which the hydrogen atoms we talked about in Rung 1—Doctor's Orders 'saturate' (or fill in, naturally, or artificially through hydrogenation in trans fats) the openings for oxygen to combine with the carbon atoms of the underlying carbohydrate molecules. Foods of animal origin contain saturated fats and should be eaten in limited quantities. Polyunsaturated fats, also called omega-6 fatty acids, are found in corn, safflower, and sunflower seed oils. Also in this category are omega-3 fatty acids, the ones in fatty fish (such as wild salmon), canola or soybean oils, walnuts, or ground flaxseed. They build cell membranes in the brain and decrease the risk of heart disease. The monounsaturated fats in olives, olive oil, nuts, coconuts, and avocados are excellent for coronary health and have even been proven to help weight loss and stabilize blood sugar.

Protein

While sugars, starches, and fats provide our fuel, our body's parts are made up of proteins, complicated strings of molecules, the basic ingredients of which are amino acids. There are two types of amino acids, those that the body produces itself and those that you can only get from food. The latter are called essential amino acids, and there are nine of them. Most animal protein includes all of the essential amino acids in addition to several others. Very few vegetables are "complete," so usually they must be combined with either animal protein or another vegetable to get all nine, which makes it a challenge for vegans and total vegetarians. Beauty-wise, insufficient protein intake displays itself in lackluster skin, dull hair, and fragile fingernails. Meanwhile, internal organs, as well as bones and brain, can suffer invisible damage.

Putting It Together

The secret to feeling great is to put these components together in the healthiest way possible. Ideally, this would mean eating more salads; brightly colored, above-ground vegetables (broccoli, spinach, kale, asparagus, green beans, peppers, cucumbers, squash, avocado, eggplant, and barley greens); organic free-range eggs; super berries (cranberries, strawberries, raspberries, and blueberries); and lean protein such as organic chicken, turkey, grass-fed beef and lamb while limiting fried food, pork, shellfish, farm-raised fish, hydrogenated oil found in commercially prepared baked goods, margarines, and processed foods, along with soft drinks, sports drinks, fruit juices, salty snacks, and sugary desserts.

Let's be realistic, here. There are days when you want to polish off that entire pepperoni pizza. As far as I'm concerned, it's perfectly okay to cheat every now and then—within reason However, just remember the affirmation that was given to me by a world-famous nutritionist: "Honey, we don't eat Italian— we *wear* Italian."(He also advised: "Don't bother to eat that bagel. Just stick it directly on your thigh, which is where it will end up, anyway!")

Know Your ABCs

To help promote your health and reduce your risk for chronic illnesses such as heart disease, certain types of cancer, type 2 diabetes, stroke, and even osteoporosis, it may be time to relearn your ABCs. In this case, that means … Aim for a good weight; Build a healthy base—eat a variety of fruit, vegetables, and whole grains; and Choose sensibly—opt for a diet that is low in saturated and trans fat, sugar, salt, and (sorry) alcohol.

Eat to Live

A principal theme in our Ladder is how holistic healing, treating the body as a whole, has often been neglected in favor of the allopathic system of simply treating symptoms. Good nutrition is very much a leading part of that paradigm. A healthy diet cannot only prevent disease, it's also an important part of any therapeutic regimen you undertake. In fact, a good diet can be more powerful than medications. The following are six prevalent diseases or conditions and how food affects them.

Cancer

Oncologists who specialize in integrative medicine stress the relationship between diet and a recurrence, and one of their theories is that cancer thrives in an acidic environment. The goal, therefore, is to slowly replace acidic foods with those that have an alkalizing effect. That means reducing your sugar intake and taking it easy on meat, dairy, refined flour, all pro cessed and packaged foods, artificial sweeteners, and alcohol. Add alkalizing fresh vegetables, such as broccoli, cabbage, and cauliflower, and fruit, particularly oranges and grapefruit, watermelon, apples, and blueberries. Take small steps. In fact, eating just one salad a day can make a noticeable difference in your health.

Many survivors with whom I've worked complain that food either never tastes the same or that they have difficulty eating and, as a result, continue to lose pounds long after their treatments have been completed. Therefore, it is important to get the appropriate vitamins and minerals to both feel better and maintain a healthy weight. Supplemental calories and meal replacements can be found in such drugstore products as Ensure and Boost. But why not make your own using nutrition powders available in health-food stores or online? They should be organic, if possible, and include protein, fiber, and probiotics, with no added sugars, hydrogenated oils, preservatives, or anything artificial. If they aren't organic, then make sure there are no pesticides or herbicides. Your body has probably been bombarded with powerful chemicals, so try to avoid taxing it with even more!

Type 2 Diabetes

The numbers are staggering—nearly 26 million children and adults in America are living with type 2 diabetes and another 79 million are pre-diabetic, which puts them at a high risk for developing the disease.

According to Dr. Howard Shapiro, author of *Eat & Beat Diabetes with Picture Perfect Weight Loss*, there are four secret weapons for not only controlling type 2 diabetes, but to beating it altogether. And those are fiber, phytonutrients, soy protein, and good fats. Here's how they work. We've already noted that soluble fiber retards the process by which sugar enters the bloodstream, reducing blood glucose spikes and helping to maintain insulin levels. Phytonutrients, the nutrients that toughen the cells of the plants (such as lycopene in tomatoes and beta-carotene in carrots), are particularly important because many of the complications of diabetes result from damage to the body's blood vessels, large and small, and these are powerhouses of blood vessel protection. Dr. Shapiro insists that "as a diabetes fighter, soy protein has no match. It helps regulate glucose and insulin levels, proactively helps weight loss, lowers the risk for cardiovascular disease and its severity, and lessens the risk for and slows the progression of kidney disease, a major complication to which patients with diabetes are particularly prone." And finally, good, monounsaturated and polyunsaturated fats decrease both total and LDL cholesterol levels, and may decrease insulin resistance.

Hypoglycemia

While we are on the topic of blood sugar, let's talk about hypoglycemia, or low blood sugar. Sometimes, bad moods, depression, nervousness, and anxiety can be attributed to what could be called the "sugar blues." As I've described earlier, our body takes the various forms of carbohydrates we ingest and breaks them down into usable glucose. If there's too much, however, insulin, a hormone made by the pancreas, kicks in and transfers the first surplus into the liver and muscles to be stored as glycogen (the object of true "carbohydrate loading"). The rest gets stored in the long-term depositories of fat cells, which is why carb-heavy foods can make anyone who doesn't need all that readily available energy—like a marathoner—pile on the pounds.

On the other hand, if you don't eat enough carbs, you risk feeling tired or light-headed. But any food or drink that produces a quick surplus of glucose could create a sense of false bravado. When the insulin clears all the excess out of the bloodstream, a sudden drop of energy caused by the resulting hypoglycemia can quickly spell despondence. This is the infamous "rollercoaster effect" that has caused many to fear that they might actually be manic-depressive, or on the verge of lunacy.

Some hypoglycemia can result from the side effects of medications or the body's physiological problems. Most, though, stems from a diet that ignores the basic rules of eating with the glycemic index value of food in mind. Make sure your meals include a spectrum of fast-burning carbs (like fresh fruit juice in the morning), medium-burning complex carbs (such as whole grains), and a lesser amount of slow-burning high protein foods (such as meat or fish). If that doesn't work, try eating a low-fat protein and a complex carbohydrate every few hours, instead of three large meals, to keep a constant level of glucose in your blood.

Gout

Gout is the most common form of arthritis in men over age 40, and it is increasingly found in women after menopause. It is caused by excess uric acid in the blood. Uric acid is the natural result of the body breaking down molecules called purines, which are found in what we eat, and can be higher in certain foods and beverages. Red meat, shellfish, certain vegetables such as asparagus, cauliflower, and mushrooms, sugary drinks, and alcohol can trigger an attack. (The Lawyer claims his rare bouts of gout don't come from the juicy steak he devoured but from the accompanying asparagus! Typical!)

In order to reduce the risk of flare-ups, here are four tips from the Gout Guidelines, recently published by the American College of Rheumatology:

- Limit table salt, which is often plentiful in sauces and gravies.
- For dessert, try cherries or even a low-sugar cherry pie. Eating cherries can reduce gout attacks by 35 percent.
- Opt for healthy snacks such as raw vegetables and pair them with a low-fat sour cream dip.
- Avoid all organ meats.

High Blood Pressure, Strokes, and Heart Disease

Since heart conditions run in my family, I have a constant fear of having a stroke or heart attack. But even a hypochondriac can't walk around with a defibrillator or count on meeting somebody on the bus who was actually paying attention in their CPR class.

The good news is you can decrease your risk for stroke and heart disease by maintaining a normal blood pressure. The basic principles are easy: Do more, eat less, and make wise food choices. The following are some nutritional recommendations from the American Heart Association:

- *Weight*—Achieving and maintaining a healthy body weight is important. If you are too heavy, losing 5 to 10 percent of your weight can greatly help lower your blood pressure.
- *Diet*—The DASH diet study, conducted by the National Heart, Lung, and Blood Institute, was the first to show that blood pressure can be lowered through diet. A DASH-style action plan means eating a diet rich in fruit, vegetables, high-fiber whole grains, low-fat dairy products, and lean meat, poultry, and fish.
- *Diet and Medication*—Don't assume that if you are taking medication for high blood pressure you no longer need to pay attention to what you eat. A healthy diet will make your medication even more effective, and may eliminate the need for it altogether.
- *Salt*—A growing body of scientific research shows a strong association between eating too much salt (sodium) and the development of high blood pressure. Consuming too much sodium can slowly damage your kidneys, and if they cannot effectively rid your body of excess fluid, your blood volume will increase, which in turn causes an increase in blood pressure. And, if you are taking medication to lower your blood pressure, too much salt could also make the drugs less effective.

- *Salt in the Food Supply*—Eighty percent of the sodium we eat comes from the salt found in commercially prepared or processed foods. Unless you cook from scratch, it's difficult to control the amount of sodium you are eating. A good first step toward lowering your intake is to read nutrition labels. Most people would be surprised to find out that bread, for example, has high sodium content. Aim for no more than 1,500 mg a day of sodium.
- *Alcohol*—A small amount of alcohol—one drink per day for women and two drinks per day for men—may be heart healthy for some people, but heavy drinking raises blood pressure in everybody.

A Slow Libido

One of my first assignments when I began my career as a health and beauty journalist was from *Cosmopolitan* magazine. The story was entitled "Nutrition to Enrich Your Sex Life." While it is long gone from my files, I remember (for some odd reason) what I included in the first paragraph: For 3,000 years or so aphrodisiacs—named for Aphrodite, the Greek goddess of love—have had a reputation for increasing male potency and female willingness. And Chinese warlords, among others seeking extra zest, sipped the original "tiger's milk." (I'll let you figure out what part of the tiger that supposedly came from.) And they did the same for bulls, sharks, rams, and rhinos.

At the time, I had asked Gaylord Hauser, one of the founding fathers of the American movement toward healthy eating, why these men risked life and limb. He said that primitive people didn't know it, but their love potions often were highly nutritious, including eggs, snails, fish, and especially oysters, all of which are full of vitamins and minerals. Therefore, they simply felt better, which undoubtedly improved their love life.

Proper nutrition was—and remains—the key to sexual vitality by keeping you healthy and fit. When you're cranky, irritable, and dependent on coffee for stimulation and wine for relaxation, you can't be a good lover—no matter how many positions you can get into. Also, many common ailments and the medications used to treat them can reduce desire and even cause erectile dysfunction, so it pays to stay well.

In addition to a balanced, heart-healthy diet, Doug Ingoldsby, known as the "Vitamin Professor," and founder of the ALL-ONE vitamin company, recommends the following specific vitamins and minerals found in certain foods and supplements that have the power to regulate the levels of sex hormones in your body, as well as the basic health of the sex glands:

- *Vitamin E*—Developed its reputation as a "sex vitamin" after laboratory tests showed that when male animals were deprived of it their testicles shrank (as The Lawyer would say, Yikes!). It increases the exchange of oxygen in the blood, which improves flow and circulation. Foods high in vitamin E include sunflower seeds, chili, almonds, dark leafy greens, and apricots.
- *Phosphorus*—New research suggests that phosphorus can amp up sex drive and responsiveness. Good sources of phosphorus are seafood, especially crabmeat and lobster, as well as eggs, wheat germ, wheat bran, legumes, nuts, and seeds.
- *Zinc*—The zinc content of the prostate gland and sperm is higher than in any other body tissues. Zinc is necessary for the production of testosterone in both men and women and helps to maintain vaginal lubrication. Zinc-rich foods include beef, lamb, eggs, whole grains, legumes, and shellfish. This may also account for the legendary effectiveness of oysters as an aphrodisiac.
- *Acetylcholine and Vitamin B$_5$ (pantothenic acid) Supplements*—Acetylcholine (ACH) is a neurotransmitter that triggers the sexual message in men and women. With too little ACH, sexual activity goes down. Choline and vitamin B$_5$ can safely and effectively enhance the body's ACH levels. You can find choline in egg yolks, nuts, soybeans, flax, sesame seeds, and cauliflower, and B$_5$ in liver, whey protein, sundried tomatoes, and avocados.
- *L-arginine*—The amino acid L-arginine, which occurs naturally in food, boosts the body's production of nitric

oxide, a compound that is considered a sensory enhancing nutrient. It's found in all proteins. The higher the protein content in a specific food, the more potent the compound.

- *Vitamins A and C, Selenium, Manganese, Linoleic Acid*—All are required for the metabolization of cholesterol, which is a basic component of hormones such as progesterone, estrogen, and testosterone. These vitamins and minerals are found in such foods as dark leafy greens, shellfish, chocolate, sunflower seeds, and citrus fruit.

Always consult your doctor before taking any supplements to be sure that they are safe in your particular situation. For example, many supplements may not be desirable for cancer patients undergoing treatment. Always ask before starting something new.

Elizabeth Somer, author of *Eat Your Way to Happiness*, maintains there is a connection between food and your state of being. In other words, eat to be happy. (And by that, I don't mean eat a Happy Meal!) Here she gives some pointers:

- *Eat regularly*—Don't attempt to skip breakfast or lunch in an effort to cut calories. You'll overeat later in the day, struggle more with mood swings and fatigue, and battle a weight problem in the long run. Be sure to eat a breakfast that includes some carbohydrates, such as cereal, fruit, and milk. For lunch, something as simple as a sandwich, nonfat milk, and a piece of fruit will fuel your brain, body, and mood.
- *Snack, but not on sweets.* Chowing down on sweets works temporarily—serotonin levels rise, and we feel better. But that high is followed by a crash. Replace these foods with more nutritious sweet treats, such as fresh sliced kiwi mixed with nonfat strawberry-kiwi yogurt, a half papaya filled with lemon yogurt, fresh fruit layered in a parfait glass and topped with a dollop of low-fat whipped cream, or nonfat milk whipped in a blender with fresh fruit and a sprinkle of nutmeg.

Diet Dilemmas

In addition to these tips for specific conditions, there are enough different diet options out there to make your head—or at least your stomach—turn. There's the one that lets you have steak and bacon, but no potatoes or bread, and another that allows potatoes and bread, but not steak and bacon. There's also the "one food a day" diet, or the "no food at all" strategy.

As anyone who has ever dieted can tell you, fad diets and strict regimens that alienate us from the basic enjoyment of food and leave us feeling empty inevitably fail. True, you may lose a few pounds at first. But it will all come back—plus about 10 more. We have also learned that sharp reductions in calories cause the body to go into a survival mode—reducing the metabolic rate to slow our need for food that isn't coming. The diet ends, and even though you now eat more sensibly, you still gain back a large chunk of the weight because your metabolic rate doesn't pick back up so quickly. That's why exercising while dieting is so important; it forces the body to continue to burn calories.

Even spas today, as opposed to years ago, have changed their programs. I recall going to one fasting place where a glass of spinach-and-beet juice was the highlight of dinner. We were starving, and food was always on our minds. So much so that when an elderly lady heard the scandal of the day—the yoga teacher was seen coming out of the tennis pro's room in the wee hours of the morning—her eyes widened in delight.

"Really?" she said, savoring the thought. "And just what do you suppose they were *eating*?"

For the most part, spa cuisine is now focused on a Mediterranean-type diet. That means primarily fish and poultry, plant-based foods, such as fruits and vegetables, whole grains, legumes, and nuts. Instead of butter, healthy fats like olive oil are featured, and herbs and spices replace salt to flavor foods. A lot has been written about the benefits of living on this type of diet. But now a new study in the *BMJ (British Medical Journal)* suggests that a Mediterranean diet can also help hinder the aging process as it is associated with longer telomere length, considered to be an indicator of slower aging. Years ago, a spa visit meant meticulously counted calories. Today the portions are normal-sized and sometimes even generous. It's no longer (just) about losing weight, it's about gaining good health along with a beautiful body.

Sadly, we can't all live at a health retreat where the food is prepared for us. If you, like most people, are confused by all the diets trumpeted as the miracle du jour, or just what might work best for you, let me explain a few of the most popular programs that reflect the current thinking in nutrition.

Gluten Free

As recently as five years ago, when you heard the word "glutens," you assumed it was referring to those big muscles in your butt. But no longer! The no-carb kick of yesteryear has now turned into the gluten-free craze of today. Glutens are proteins found naturally in wheat and related grains, and generally give breads, for example, their chewy quality, since the name comes from the Latin word for glue.

What we know is that people with celiac disease (an actually quite rare autoimmune disorder of the small intestine) are physically intolerant to gluten. That begs the question: If you don't have celiac disease, do you really need to avoid gluten? Or have we fallen prey (again) to all the hype? Is there any way to know?

If you believe you are having trouble digesting gluten, nutritionist Isabel De Los Rios, cofounder of BeyondDiet.com, suggests eliminating gluten from your diet for at least four to six weeks to determine whether your symptoms are alleviated. Since those who are sensitive to gluten often have problems with lactose, cut out dairy and dairy-containing products as well.

Gluten-containing foods and ingredients to avoid include the obvious—wheat, wheat germ, barley, rye, pasta, spelt, cold cereals (not all—read the ingredients), semolina, and hydrolyzed vegetable protein. The not-so-obvious are beer, oats (in their pure form, oats are gluten-free, but it is very possible, perhaps common, that they have been contaminated somewhere during processing with wheat or other gluten-containing grains), and even soy sauce. Allowable gluten-free substitutes are uncontaminated oats and oatmeal, amaranth, arrowroot, buckwheat, millet, quinoa, bean flours (such as garbanzo, sorghum), and rice. And, of course, supermarket shelves are now filled with gluten-free choices.

But buyers beware: Many products advertised as gluten-free are not necessarily healthier. They may be processed with hydrogenated oils or other evils. And the ones promoted for children could be loaded with sugar. According to Isabel, here's what a gluten-free wannabe can do:

- Bake your own breads, muffins, and cookies made from coconut flour, almond flour, rice flour, or bean flours. This is also an option for gluten-free children who want to eat the same foods as their peers. Remember to allow your children to participate in the baking process, and they will love eating their healthy creations.
- Purchase cereals made from quinoa and millet instead of wheat or oats (again, unless certified as gluten-free).
- Focus more on healthy proteins (organic eggs, grass-fed beef, free-range poultry, wild-caught fish), healthy fats (coconut oil, raw nuts, avocados) and an assortment of fruits and vegetables instead of buying processed "gluten-free" foods.

Anti-inflammatory

Recent studies conclude that inflammation in the artery walls (leading to plaque and subsequently blockages) is a major contributor to heart disease, as well as strokes, diabetes, and obesity. Inflammation, the same as fevering—all based on heat, ergo the flame in inflammation—is part of our body's own defense system. By launching into a full-blown attack, our white cells and chemicals create redness and swelling to kill such unwelcomed invaders as bacteria, toxins, and viruses.

Chronic inflammation, though, is just as harmful as the acute type is beneficial.

An anti-inflammatory diet is important for those of us with conditions that are based upon or worsened by inflammation, such as arthritis. Some of the foods known to foster inflammation are caffeine, alcohol, food additives, refined sugar, refined flour, corn, soy, gluten, dairy, and even eggs. Dr. Aimée Shunney, a naturopathic physician in Santa Cruz, California, who specializes in women's health, functional endocrinology, and family medicine, says to be sure to include foods that have anti-inflammatory properties, such as fatty fish, flaxseeds, hemp seeds, and walnuts, as well as plenty of monounsaturated fatty acids. Fish oil supplements also provide anti-inflammatory benefits for the circulatory system.

"Also make sure you are eating good-quality lean protein," she continues. "Too much red meat can be inflammatory, so limit that to no more than a few times a month. Instead, focus on vegetarian sources of protein such as nuts, seeds and fish, plus lean chicken and turkey. You also want complex carbohydrates, including whole, non-gluten grains such as millet and buckwheat. Fruit and vegetables provide vitamins and minerals. Green tea has anti-inflammatory properties, as does a little bit of dark chocolate, red wine, and even beer (the hops in beer have a profound anti-inflammatory effect). Fermented foods have good bacteria that help with digestion, and good digestion means low inflammation."

Sugar Free

When The Big Apple's ex-mayor sought to regulate our behavior by prohibiting stores and fast-food chains from either serving or selling sugary drinks in containers larger than 16 ounces, New Yorkers went wild. Some citizens referred to him as the "Mayortollah," the "Nanny who never sleeps," or even a "Soda Jerk!" His bid was eventually defeated, but the problem still remains. A recent survey shows that nearly one in four New Yorkers is obese. And similar figures continue to rise in outrageous proportions throughout the country. The number extends to overweight kids who are doomed to shorter lives, filled with serious diseases such as type 2 diabetes, cancer, and coronary thrombosis, making them the first generation whose parents may actually be expected to outlive them.

The main culprit is sugar. Sugar is ubiquitous—and highly addictive. And it's not just found in sodas, cakes, cookies, candy, and other sweets. It's added to many processed foods such as ketchup, bread, soup, cereal, peanut butter, cured meat, and salad dressing.

Per the New Hampshire Department of Health and Human Services (NH DHHS): Two hundred years ago, the average American ate only two pounds of sugar a year. In 1970, that number rose to 123 pounds. Now, according to the Centers for Disease Control and Prevention, the average American consumes almost 160 pounds of sugar per year, which is equal to three pounds (or six cups) of sugar each week!

The first step is to watch for sugar hidden in processed and packaged foods. Second, replace sugary snacks and drinks with healthier choices. Here are a few alternatives to high-sugar food, courtesy of the NH DHHS: Instead of soda, try 100 percent fruit juice mixed with seltzer, or flavored or plain seltzers. Substitute candy bars with fresh or dried fruit, raw vegetables such as carrots and red peppers, or dry, unsweetened cereal mixed with dried fruit. Replace cookies and cakes with graham crackers, animal crackers, vanilla wafer cookies, or a crunchy fruit such as an apple or a pear. Swap ice cream for frozen juice pops (100 percent juice), a small serving of a low-fat frozen yogurt topped with sliced berries, or a smoothie made with yogurt and berries.

Vegan

My friend Abby told me that she became a vegan because she found it abhorrent to eat anything that had parents—or a face. Truth be told, that seemed a little, well, over the top. Then one day I was in a fish store when I heard a faint squeaky sound. Looking down, I could have sworn the source was the live soft shell crabs as they inched about in the display case. I felt so guilty that I was contemplating eating their neighbors, the shrimp, that I couldn't look them in the eye(s). Since then, I've never consumed another crustacean. But that's as far as I've gone.

Many people think vegan is just short for vegetarian. While true vegans do eat a lot of vegetables, they try to avoid everything that may come from animals. That means no meat, fish, dairy, or eggs. Furthermore, the stricter ones won't even eat honey or wear clothing or shoes made from wool, silk, or leather.

Kathy Freston, the *New York Times* best-selling author of *The Lean* and health and wellness activist, suggests a few tips on "leaning in" to a plant-based diet:

- *Set Your Intention*—But don't expect it to make a significant change all at once. You must gradually make the shift.
- *Don't Deprive*—The hardest part of beginning a plant-based diet is that people are hesitant to give up their traditional favorite foods, such as burgers and pizza, or a feast on Thanksgiving. So they feel left out and unfulfilled. You don't have to give those things up completely, though; you can just have vegan versions, such as veggie burgers, pizza made with nondairy cheese and veggie sausage, and meat-alternative turkey with mashed potatoes made with soy milk and nondairy butter.
- *Eat an Apple a Day*—The fiber fills you up and keeps your blood sugar steady. The pectin from apples, a soluble fiber, is actually twice as good as other fiber, because it leaves your stomach twice as slowly, so you feel full longer.
- *Drink Eight Glasses (At Least) of Water a Day*—It's called preloading. In one study, people who drink two cups of water before meals lost five pounds more fat in a

12-week period than people who didn't drink water. And they changed nothing else!

- *Add Two Tablespoons of Ground Flaxseeds to Your Food Daily*—For example, in a smoothie or soup. Its soluble fiber adds volume to your food and fills you up. And flax has a powerful antioxidant in it called lignans, which has shown to be a cancer preventative.
- *Switch Up Your Milk*—It's easy to switch out dairy for milks made of almond, rice, hemp, soy, or coconut. There's no loss, except for the pounds that come off as a result. Plus many of the nondairy milks on the market have 50 percent more calcium than dairy milk.
- *Eat a Hearty, Fiber-Filled Breakfast*—Steel-cut oatmeal or a bowl of brown rice with chopped dates and almonds with some hot nondairy milk poured atop. This will kick start your metabolism and keep you from overeating later in the day.

Since eating this way, Kathy has reached her ideal weight and stayed there. She added, "I haven't had so much as a cold in 10 years. My skin has cleared up (I had acne way into my adulthood). But most of all, I feel good in my soul, like something in me is aligned and on target with my best self. Not only am I exercising my muscle of compassion, but I also am happy about being a good steward for the environment, since animal agriculture is so detrimental to the water, soil, forests, and air."

Just Juice

On almost every other street in Manhattan you'll find a bar touting fresh juices. But is the juice worth the squeeze, as they say? To me, it's certainly a better way to go than Burger King. To The Lawyer, it's a shameful waste of good real estate, but he does listen to the experts (other than his wife!). So I asked Dr. Michael T. Murray, author of *The Complete Book of Juicing, Revised and Updated: Your Delicious Guide to Youthful Vitality*, to answer a few of my pressing questions.

Why juice? Isn't it better to just eat the whole fruit or vegetable?

Dr. Murray: If you think about it, the body actually converts the foods we eat into juice so the nutrients can be easily absorbed. So juicing it before you consume it saves the body energy, resulting in increased vitality. It also delivers more soluble fiber faster and in an easier-to-digest form.

A lot of bottled juices claim to contain vitamins and minerals. Is fresh always preferable?

Dr. Murray: Yes! Fresh juice contains many more vitamins, minerals, and other nutritional compounds, such as enzymes and flavonoids, than its canned or bottled counterparts, which have been cooked (pasteurized) to keep them on the shelves longer. Cooking can cause the loss of up to 97 percent of water-soluble vitamins (B and C), and up to 40 percent of the fat-soluble vitamins (A, D, E, and K).

Do homemade juices have increased antioxidant and anticancer properties as well?

Dr. Murray: They do! In fact, a study comparing commercial apple juice with freshly juiced apples found that fresh, raw juice had more antiviral compounds than the store-bought versions. Another study found that fresh, raw apple juice and berry juice (especially raspberries and blackberries) have more ellagic acid, a potent anticancer and antioxidant compound that is stripped from juice when it has been processed.

I've heard that some fresh juices also help get rid of toxins. How do they work?

Dr. Murray: Speaking just of fresh fruit juice, fruit contains ample glutathione, a small protein composed of three amino acids, which are also manufactured in our cells, which aid in the detoxification of heavy metals such as lead, as well as the elimination of pesticides and solvents.

What impact does raw juicing have on weight loss?

Dr. Murray: To begin with, it's a phenomenal way to reach the goal of ingesting 60 percent of total calories from raw foods. Diets containing a high percentage (up to 60 percent of calories) of uncooked foods are associated with significant weight loss and lowering of blood pressure in overweight individuals.

How about a quick recipe that would appeal to everyone? (Read: The Lawyer!)

Dr. Murray: For a delicious, nutritious fruit juice, put two whole apples, sliced in quarters, and one-half cup each of raspberries and blackberries through a juicer. Drink it up right away for a blast of energy and nutrients.

Bringing It Home

Whether or not you keep a juicer in your kitchen, eating in is generally healthier than eating out. By cooking at home, you can control the amount of fat, sugar, and sodium, as well as portion size. Of course, the problem is it takes less time and effort to pick up the phone and order a pizza than to make a proper dinner. Sadly, I fear that my kid's fondest memories of my cuisine are those little white take-out boxes of General Tso's chicken, which I ordered when I was too overwhelmed to cook dinner. But cooking at home doesn't have to be difficult. Ted Allen, renowned cookbook author and Food Network star, offers some advice for us duffers on home cooking:

- *Safety First*—Never leave meat—or any food that needs refrigeration—at room temperature for more than two hours.

- **Essential Utensils**—You might not need a candy ther-
  mometer or a tagine, unless you love Moroccan cooking.
  But a versatile stand mixer is always useful to have on
  hand. A good rule of thumb is to not buy anything that
  only does one thing. Or anything gimmicky—such as a
  hot-dog cooker or an indoor marshmallow roaster. Good
  for starters are an eight-inch chef's knife, a few soft cut-
  ting boards made of plastic or wood, a sauté pan, a two-
  quart and three-quart saucepan, maybe a grill pan, some
  cookie sheets, wooden spoons, especially with flat edges
  for scraping, a few spatulas, and a good peeler. (After a
  quick inventory, I'm proud to say I have at least two of
  those.)
- **Herb Store**—Nothing enhances taste like fresh herbs.
  Keep tender herbs such as parsley, tarragon, or cilantro
  fresh by wrapping them in damp paper towels and plac-
  ing them in unsealed plastic bags in the fridge. Thyme
  and rosemary should be stored dry in the fridge. Basil
  can be frozen if it's chopped and blended into olive oil as
  pesto.
- **Fresh vs. Frozen**—Some frozen vegetables are healthier than fresh because they are flash-frozen right at the
  source, thereby losing fewer nutrients than those that
  need to travel farther to market. They are also great
  alternatives for ones that are out of season. Remember,
  though, some freeze better than others—corn, peas, and
  green beans, for example, are good, but not asparagus.

Making extra portions and freezing them for busy nights is
another good way to avoid the take-out trap. And remember,
healthy doesn't need to be complicated.

The Fallacy of the Calorie

Although, as we've discussed, it's not how much you weigh, but
how you feel, some of us are constantly battling, especially as
we get older, what my English friend calls our "wiggly bits."

And that calls for losing weight. Don't count calories, though. Just make sure you eat enough healthy food to fill you up and satisfy you, so you don't go on that yo-yo syndrome. I also never advocate doing it quickly. Think of it this way: If you only lose one pound a week, that's still fifty-two pounds a year. Conversely, if you gain that pound, in well less than two years' time, you would be obese.

To share some no-nonsense tactics with us, I have invited Steve Siebold, author of *Die Fat or Get Tough: 101 Differences in Thinking Between Fat People and Fit People*, to weigh in.

Steve says that 99 percent compliance on a diet is still failure. "It sounds harsh, but if you're going to get fit, it's all or nothing." Steve believes that there are no shortcuts to dieting. You either adhere to a healthy diet or pay the price of gaining weight, sickness, and disease. "Remember, this is not a short-term project. It's a lifetime strategy that is essential and must be approached like any other long-term investment." Here are a few of his suggestions:

- Expect challenges such as cravings, and when this happens, have a plan in place to push forward and stay compliant.
- Create a vision board filled with pictures of lean sexy people (I've told The Lawyer that the Victoria's Secret Angels calendar doesn't qualify). Hang it in a very visible location (though perhaps not in your office). When you get discouraged and want to give up, get the urge to eat or cheat on your diet, look at the vision board.
- Before you put anything in your mouth, always ask yourself, "How is this food going to impact my health?"
- Developing a "self-talk" to keep you on track may be the greatest mental toughness tool of all. This is one of the things that will really help you change your core beliefs about diets and exercise, and help you make it through times like any holiday.
- Realize that ultimately being fit and healthy is completely your responsibility, and don't put the blame on others

or anything else, including restaurants and the food manufacturers.

- Work through your food/eating challenges with a friend. When you have someone else to help hold you accountable, it makes the process much easier.
- Try to avoid turning to food for comfort. Take at least 30 minutes each day for yourself. Go for a walk. Do anything you enjoy. Just make some time for you.
- There is no shame in saying "No" (nicely) when someone wants you to try their homemade dessert. Simply tell people that you're watching what you eat because you are trying to lose weight and get healthy.
- Be wary of what you drink. Water will help fill you up so you eat less. On the other hand, cocktails are packed with calories and even too much wine could loosen you up to the point where you forget about your diet.
- When you are tempted to cheat, ask yourself these questions: "When am I going to stop starting over? What makes tomorrow better than today to get fit? If I continue to cheat and start over, will I eventually die fat?"

Steve's way may be a little too tough for even me, but clearly dying obese isn't anyone's objective!

Food for Thought

Indeed, the purpose of this book is to help you do everything you can to look and feel Better Than Before—forever more. For most of us, that means working incrementally, not all-out all the time. With that in mind, here are my favorite practical tips for healthy eating:

- ***Drink Up***—Water, that is. Coffee, tea, juice, and soda don't count. Drink water regularly, even if you aren't thirsty. And if you don't like the taste, squeeze some lemon (or lime) into it.

- *You Can't Eat What You Can't See*—Go on a junk hunt by reading the nutrition labels of everything in your kitchen and tossing out everything that isn't healthy or will beckon you to indulge.
- *If It's White Don't Take a Bite*—Cut all "white foods" out of your diet. Those include white bread, white pasta, white sugar, white flour, white rice, and white potatoes. Replace them with whole grain foods.
- *To Satisfy a Snack Attack*—Try unbuttered, unsalted popcorn (make sure it's air popped); raw (not salted or candied) almonds; or a piece (not the whole bar, mind you) of dark chocolate, which is a good source of mono-unsaturated fats and high in antioxidants. Your refrigerator should also contain probiotic yogurt and organic apples and pears. A frozen banana dipped in dark chocolate with a few chopped almonds sprinkled over the top makes a great treat.
- *Read Labels*—When you shop, be sure to check all labels for chemical additives. Basic rule: If you can't pronounce it, don't buy it! (One exception: quinoa.) Registered dietitian Rachel K. Johnson, a professor at the University of Vermont and spokesperson for the American Heart Association, suggests looking for whole grains as the first ingredients. Be aware of the amount of saturated fat and sodium in what you buy. "Sodium intake should be kept at 1,500 mg—about two-thirds of a teaspoon of salt—and saturated fats should be only about 7 percent of your daily calorie intake."
- *Stay Away from Sodas*—Keep sugary drinks—including sodas, energy and fruit drinks, sweetened iced teas and lemonade—off your shopping list. Diet soda is no better than regular. The chemicals in them actually trigger your sweet tooth, which can make you want more. Instead, pour about an inch of the original into a glass and fill the rest up with seltzer.
- *Take It Easy*—You don't have to jump right into a diet full of legumes, flaxseed, goat yogurt, and broccoli sprouts.

Always include the foods you like; otherwise, you will never stay on any program. Have fun with it. For example, try a new color fruit or vegetable each day or week.

- *Organic Is Generally Better*—However, if everything organic is too expensive, simply pick one or two things that you like to eat in quantity and buy those organic, especially dairy products, apples, celery, tomatoes, cucumbers, and berries. One of the hallmarks of organic food is the lack of pesticides, and most of these are sprayed on the outside of fruit and vegetables.

- *One Small Step*—For a start, just make one small change a day. For example, substitute a slice of whole grain bread for white. If you want pizza, order a vegetable topping.

- *Eat Like an Athlete*—Do what all the superstar athletes do—start your day with a good, healthy breakfast that includes protein, carbohydrates, and fiber. For example, an omelet with one egg yolk and two whites, and a slice of whole grain toast. Furthermore, a new study published in the *Nutrition Journal* found that eating a bowl of oatmeal helps you feel full longer and may reduce the likeliness of grabbing a snack or overeating at your next meal. If time is an issue, whip up a quick smoothie with yogurt, a banana, frozen fruit, chocolate protein powder, natural almond butter, and ice.

- *Eat Local*—"There are many good reasons to eat locally produced foods; the first among them is that they're very good for us," says interventional cardiologist and professional chef Michael S. Fenster, M.D., author of *Eating Well, Living Better*. "There's a direct relationship between our food, our environment, our genetics, and our health. Eating locally grown foods gives us our most nutritious meals, most flavorful meals."

- *Keep a Record of Your Progress*—By doing so, you commit on paper and then confront what you see or do. Also, write positive affirmations and prominently place them where they will motivate you—your bathroom mirror, the scale, the refrigerator or closet door.

The Tip of the Iceberg (Lettuce)

We have reached the end of this rung. Your true motivator, the takeaway message, if you will, is that just by making a few simple changes in your daily eating plan you will feel markedly Better Than Before. Remember: Your health is directly related to what you put in your mouth. As we continue our climb up the ladder, know too that even if you eat everything right and are at a good weight, you still need to exercise, which is why our next rung is "Fitness."

Key Concepts from
Rung 3—Nutrition

Concept _____

Why It Interests Me _____

_____

_____

_____

_____

How could I apply it to my life? _____

_____

_____

_____

_____

Concept _____

Why It Interests Me _____

_____

_____

_____

_____

How could I apply it to my life? _____

_____

_____

_____

_____

Concepts to Share

Concept _____

_____

_____

_____

With Whom? _____

_____

_____

_____

Concept _____

_____

_____

_____

With Whom? _____

_____

_____

_____

Concept _____

_____

_____

_____

With Whom? _____

_____

_____

_____

Fitness

Higher, Faster, Stronger

—The Olympic motto

Fit for Life

Being physically fit is basically a no-brainer. It's not like anyone will argue they are better off being in *worse* shape! All of us are aware by now—or at least we should be—that exercise controls weight, combats disease, improves your mood, boosts your energy, and promotes better sleep. And we don't have to be competing in, say, the Red Bull Cliff Diving championships to reap cardiovascular benefits. But that's where the consensus ends and the disputes begin. How hard should I work out? How often? Should I run, swim, play tennis, lift weights, or all of the above? Should I join a gym, buy weights to use at home, get up early and exercise, or later at night? Alas, too often that leads to "Oh well, I'll decide next week." Then like the diet that starts with good intentions and ends with the first sniff of a bacon cheeseburger, you promise yourself that you'll start your exercise program on Monday. And then, of course, something comes up and you push it off until the next week … then the next. You know the drill!

That being said, in Rung 3—Nutrition I talked about how proper nutrition gives you the right fuel and the best building blocks for good health. But even a new Ferrari will sputter and break down if it isn't driven properly and often. So no matter if you eat enough leafy greens, whole grains, and organic pasta to fill a Whole Foods truck, you still have to exercise. If you don't, two unhealthy things can happen. If you are ingesting normal amounts, the extra glucose in your bloodstream will be stored away as fat, thanks to our insulin. And if you're on a diet, the body will automatically go into survival mode and reduce its metabolic rate—so when you start eating normally, your body will treat even less calories than before as excess and then turn that into fat. (Are you noticing a theme here?)

The other side of the equation is that we need muscles to accomplish pretty much everything—even your eyes move around using muscles. And as the *Wall Street Journal* has reported, we start losing body strength after age 40. According to Nathan LeBrasseur, the director of the Muscle Performance and Physical Function Laboratory and the Healthy Aging and Independent Living Initiative at the Mayo Clinic, most people will lose approximately 30 percent of their muscle mass over their lifetime and as much as 50 percent by the time they reach their 90s. And what does the *Wall Street Journal* say is the solution? After discussing advanced research into such things as myostatins, it concludes that "the best medicine available to maintain muscle mass and strength is less complicated and costly—namely, exercise and a healthy diet." Big surprise!

If that's not enough to get you moving, let me provide you with even more motivation by discussing how exercise can help us avoid or minimize some common health conditions.

The (Heart) Beat Goes On

Every cardiologist worth his EKG machine will tell you that active people are nearly half as likely to get heart disease and strokes as their sedentary counterparts. After all, your heart is a muscle; and it gets stronger and healthier if you are physically fit. Cardiovascular capacity and its air intake relative, pulmonary capacity, are far and away the most important therapeutic elements of exercise. What could possibly be more important than how hard your heart has to work to pump blood through your system, and how efficiently and easily you can bring your body's fuel and oxygen throughout your body?

Therefore, a sensible heart-healthy program should include "cardio" (the aerobic activities that raise your heart rate to burn calories, keep your blood pressure in check, lower your LDL cholesterol, and boost your HDL); stretching, to make your muscles more flexible and reduce the likelihood of injury; and strength training, two to three times a week using weights, resistance bands, or your own body weight (think yoga and Pilates). From Rung 1—Doctor's Orders, you already know that the American Heart Association recommends being active five to six days a week, 20 to 30 minutes at a time, aiming for a total of at least 150 minutes of moderate-to-vigorous activity a week.

And it's never too late to start. Even taking a brisk walk for 30 minutes a day can make a difference. "No need to run a marathon, unless you want to!" says Allan S. Stewart, M.D., director of Aortic Surgery and codirector of the Valve Center in the Department of Cardiothoracic Surgery at The Mount Sinai Hospital in New York City. "Oftentimes it takes a 'wake up' call to lead us to a healthier lifestyle. I received one from a former patient, urging me to run a triathlon with him one year after his heart surgery. We did—he beat me!—and so began a new start for me, an overweight middle-aged heart surgeon." Stewart lost 30 pounds and now serves as an example to his patients to use a traumatic event "as a springboard" to a healthier lifestyle.

Fitness and wellness expert Dr. Lynn Romejko Jacobs of Southern Methodist University adds: "I have worked in cardiac rehab, and it was so inspirational to see people who had all kinds of coronary challenges—by-pass surgery, heart attacks, high blood pressure—actually get better and become more healthy and fit through exercise. There is a preponderance of evidence, and there is no doubt in my mind, that exercise can strengthen your heart, lungs, and blood vessels."

Every Step Counts

"Staying active to keep your heart as healthy as possible is essential," says Dr. Julie Silver, an associate professor at Harvard Medical School in the Department of Physical Medicine and Rehabilitation, and author of *You Can Heal Yourself*. "Though it may seem trivial, walking is a relatively complex process that helps improve balance, strength, and endurance throughout the body."

Get a pedometer, she suggests, and begin to record how many steps you are taking each day. At first, all you are doing is figuring out how active you are during the day. With this as your baseline, you can set short-term and long-term goals that involve increasing the number of steps you take. Usually, a reasonable initial short-term goal is to increase the average number of steps by 1,000 steps per day. "The goal for active, healthy people is 10,000 steps per day, so consider this number when you are making your long-term goals."

Cancer and Exercise

The association between fitness and heart disease is well-known; however, the latest medical research shows beyond question that an exercise program is invaluable in helping to keep cancer from returning. Yet, three-fourths of survivors are not meeting the recommendations for physical activity set by the U.S. Department of Health and Human Services' Agency for Healthcare Research and Quality.

The agency's report on the effectiveness of exercise concluded that physical activity can both improve a survivor's physiological and psychosocial health and effectively fight post-cancer fatigue. Its most important finding was that regular exercise boosts your immune system. It also releases endorphins and brain proteins or modulators, which stimulate brain cells to help you feel better and improve your concentration, mood, memory, and happiness. By increasing serotonin, the "happiness" hormone, exercise plays a crucial role in relieving depression and anxiety, all the while building up a healthy appetite, stronger bones, and sex drive. In other words, all the things that cancer may have slowed down will be revved up. Aside from boosting the body's immune system, exercise has now been proved to reduce mortality and the risk for recurrent breast cancer by approximately 50 percent and colon cancer by 60 percent.

Dr. Kerry S. Courneya, professor and Canada Research Chair in Physical Activity and Cancer at the University of Alberta in Edmonton, adds: "Exercise is important for breast cancer survivors because it helps them get through treatments, recover after treatments, and improves their quality of life." In one study, Courneya and his colleagues found that exercise during chemotherapy, especially weight training, helps breast cancer patients complete more of their treatments, which may reduce their risk for recurrence. The evidence for the benefits of exercise is so strong that the American Cancer Society, the American College of Sports Medicine, and many other cancer agencies endorse exercise programs for breast cancer survivors.

"Studies show that physical activity actually causes the skeletal muscles to communicate to other tissues and can literally affect cell transformation," says Dr. Jack Eck, an internal medical physician at the Shaw Regional Cancer Center near Vail, Colorado. "We now know the science behind physical activity and understand that these cell changes protect against metabolic disease, including cancer and osteoporosis, which can be a side-effect of cancer treatment."

Breathe Easy

The importance of pulmonary capacity, which we talked about in connection with heart health, is even more important for asthma and other chronic obstructive pulmonary disease (COPD) sufferers. But for them, extra care must be taken in developing an exercise regime, since overdoing it can bring on an attack. Even so, asthma is not an excuse to avoid exercise; on the contrary, it's a reason to work out intelligently to help you overcome its debilitating effects. Such superstar athletes as four-time Olympian Jackie Joyner-Kersee and NFL running back Jerome Bettis never let asthma stop them!

First, though, be sure to check with your physician to see if you have exercise-induced asthma. If so, follow his or her instructions carefully. And always take your inhaler with you. If outdoor air quality is poor from pollution or a high pollen count, stay indoors. If you feel symptoms or shortness of breath at any time, stop and rest. Walking, cycling, and swimming are the best forms of exercise for pulmonary and bronchial health since they are aerobic (meaning that you don't have to work so hard that your body can't use the ongoing amount of oxygen you are breathing) and totally scalable; that is, they are adjustable over time to increase intensity simply by going faster and/or longer. If you are just beginning or you've been sedentary for some time, start with a short session. Even 10 minutes is better than nothing. But if you keep at it, again staying attuned to your body, you will be able to do more over time, making you both fitter and increasing the very lung and bronchial capacity that will limit your asthma or COPD problems.

Similarly, there are numerous studies and testimonials that prove that regular exercise can improve or help resolve seasonal allergies. Most allergy sufferers are dealing with congestion and inflammation that interfere with oxygen flow from the mouth and nose to the lungs. They often feel sick with flulike symptoms, so they don't want to exercise—but that's exactly what they *should* do. In addition to drinking more water and not eating foods that cause allergic reactions, working out helps move allergens through the body so that they can be eliminated through the skin and kidneys. You may find it helpful to train indoors when pollen levels are high—they peak from 5 AM to 10 AM—to reduce exposure. Be sure, too, to breathe through your nose as much as you can to help filter any allergens.

Antianxiety and Stress

As we touched on in Rung 2—Emotional Well-Being, exercise helps alleviate stress in many ways. The simplest is by giving you a socially acceptable way to vent. Each time I interview athletes, I am always surprised to find out how sweet and soft-spoken some of the guys who are the most violent on the field or ice seem to be. That's because they have found a way to release their stress. When your nervous system has trouble dealing with the slings and arrows life tosses our way, we need to find a way to convert that pent-up frustration. After all, evolution has hardwired us to react to anger or a feeling of being threatened—whether by a woolly mammoth, an evil manager, or an overbearing mother-in-law—by a surge of adrenaline and the desire to fight or flee. When modern society prevents you from doing either, the frustration is natural and unavoidable. A good hard run or a tough workout at the gym can replace taking flight or getting into a fight.

Also, the biochemistry of high stress levels is now well-understood. Whenever you're in danger—or just super frazzled—your hypothalamus shoots cortisol, a stress hormone, into your bloodstream. It quickens your heartbeat, feeds your brain extra oxygen, and unleashes energy from your fat and glycogen stores—all good things if you are being chased by a bear. But chronically high levels undermine memory and may lead to permanent changes in the brain. Additionally, excessive cortisol has been linked with major depression, osteoporosis (it extracts calcium and other minerals from bones and interferes with the laying down of new bone), high blood pressure, and insulin resistance. Just three hours a week of cardio or weight training considerably reduces cortisol levels, especially if you keep your workouts short and sweaty. "When you exercise for longer than 40 minutes, your cortisol starts to rise again," says naturopathic physician Natasha Turner, N.D., author of *The Hormone Diet*. "Go for intense, interval-based routines such as alternating jogging and sprinting for 60 seconds each, for 30 minutes total."

Research has found that the long-term benefits of exercise include the generation of cell growth in the brain to reduce the intensity of stress response in all situations. Exercise encourages good oxygen flow to the brain, which promotes effective information processing. A mere 20 to 30 minutes a day—even split into 10-minute segments—a few days a week will help ease anxiety and elevate your mood—and help keep your brain healthy!

Obesity

Here's a sobering fact from the World Health Organization: For the first time in human history, more people will die from obesity than hunger and starvation. As we discussed in Rung 3—Nutrition, being overweight increases your risk for type 2 diabetes, high blood pressure, heart disease, stroke, osteoarthritis, and cancer.

Exercise is critical for weight management in three ways: First is the simple math that you lose weight by burning more calories than you consume (minus the energy it takes to digest it). So the more you force your muscles to work, the more calories of fuel it takes to operate your engine, and the greater the possible differential between intake and what you use. This in turn forces the body to rely on its stored energy—our fat deposits. The second way is what we talked about earlier. Exercising regularly prevents a dieter's body from dropping to a survival-level metabolic rate. By keeping your metabolism at normal or, as you get in shape, even higher rates, you ensure that when you stop dieting, you won't just put the weight back on, even though you are eating less than before. And finally, scientists have proven that muscle tissue needs more calories, even at rest, than fat stored in your body. So, muscle-building exercise is the healthy gift that keeps on giving. Even while you are sleeping, it is working to turn your caloric intake versus burn rate in your favor!

Arthritis

If the thought of getting up and moving around on your aching knees or bending over using that bad back makes you avoid exercise, think again! "It may seem counterintuitive, but one of the most effective methods for decreasing joint pain and stiffness is regular exercise," says Marc Perry, a former Division I athlete at Yale University and founder and CEO of the popular fitness resource site BuiltLean.com. Research has shown that exercise can increase bone density, keep joints stable, improve joint function and flexibility, decrease pain, and improve balance. For best results, your exercise routine should incorporate resistance training (free weights, machines, or resistance bands), low-impact aerobics (brisk walking, cycling, or swimming), and stretching. If you are experiencing substantial pain, consider swimming or water aerobics, which provides resistance with very little impact.

Diabetes

According to the American Diabetes Association, in addition to the 26 million Americans who have diabetes, there are 79 million in a state of pre-diabetes. "You can develop type 2 diabetes even if you're at an ideal weight," says Dr. Brett Osborn, a board-certified neurosurgeon and author of *Get Serious: A Neurosurgeon's Guide to Optimal Health and Fitness*. "Excess sugar—and the surplus of insulin it produces—damages and constricts the walls of your blood vessels, leading to cellular deterioration, internal inflammation, and a host of other deleterious conditions."

We now know that exercise depends upon the glucose in your blood for fuel. In other words, it helps reduce the need for insulin—but cannot eliminate it entirely—by working to keep blood sugar levels lower simply by using it. Says celebrity trainer Gunnar Peterson, whose clients have included Halle Berry, Jennifer Lopez, Kim Kardashian, Sophia Vergara, and numerous NBA and NFL stars, to name a few: "While exercise may not be a cure for diabetes, it certainly helps in a big way. Not only does it lower blood pressure, but it has been shown to control and reduce blood glucose levels, which are the source of energy in our bodies. Furthermore, exercise strengthens your heart and increases insulin receptors in your red blood cells, as well as lowering insulin resistance. Strength training, in particular, increases muscle and reduces fat."

Please, though, work with your doctor to make sure that your insulin injections are coordinated with your exercise program so they work together best.

A Lagging Libido

While technically not a malady, poor sexual desire and performance probably weigh more on our minds than many other conditions. Of course, regular physical activity can leave you feeling energized and looking better, on or off the treadmill, which may have a positive effect on your sex life. But there's more to it than that.

Research shows that increased physical activity can lead to enhanced arousal for women, and that men who exercise regularly are less likely to have problems with erectile dysfunction than those who don't. As far as having a positive psychological effect on your sex life, scientists are able to explain this emotional boost by the hormones and neurotransmitters released during a workout. Exercise releases mood-elevating serotonin and endorphins, one of which is oxytocin, known as the "love" hormone. Not only does oxytocin itself lead to relaxation, it pulls double-duty by working against the stress hormone, cortisol.

Also, for most men, simple cardiovascular exercise affects levels of testosterone, the hormone that makes them more, well, manly. But, for maximum testosterone production, work out your largest muscle groups, like legs and back, to the point where those muscles are completely fatigued. Squats and lunges holding free weights and high-resistance bike spins are two examples of exercises that can result in an immediate testosterone boost.

No Ifs, Ands—or Butts

Above all, exercise is really the only way to develop your muscles. That alone will make your body function better, the very definition of good health. Maintaining muscle mass as we age can also help us prevent falls and other injuries. So, how do we get started, and most important, how do we stick with it?

Granted, unless you are a committed gym rat, seasoned athlete, or dedicated weekend warrior, exercising regularly isn't the easiest habit to adopt. It's not because we don't begin with good intentions. For example, my colleague Lorraine joined a health club, set on making it a regular part of her weekly routine. She carefully selected the right gym clothes, a headband, sneakers, and music for her iPod, and off she went, determined to prove to all her doubting friends that this time she was serious about getting into shape. Very proud of herself, she set the leg-press machine at a level that seemed a good challenge. One push into her 10-rep set she heard a popping sound coming from her hamstring. She never went back. Having already paid her six-month membership, it became the world's most expensive leg press.

Lorraine made one classic mistake—overdoing it too soon. She is certainly not alone. Others make another common error—they bargain with themselves. For example, "I worked out, so now I can eat that (fill in the blank, and make it super fattening and unhealthy)." And then they wonder why they never seem to make any progress.

I've found that the best motivations for exercise are to be smart about your program before you start it, make it as much fun and flexible as possible, and to be attuned to how much you are improving. Because once you feel better—not to mention look better—you won't want to stop.

The best approach is to make it fun by finding a program that you enjoy! You can choose from spinning, cardio, Zumba, weight training, Pilates, martial arts, and yoga, to name but a few. And while single-purpose gyms are still by far the largest segment of the industry, a new generation of multipurpose fitness facilities is becoming available, led by Life Time Fitness with its more than 100 all-in-one exercise and sports centers that provide an entire spectrum of fitness options in one club. Just remember, unless you really want to exercise, you won't. So pick one you like, or try a few until you do.

All my experts—and basic logic—agree that getting in good shape is like giving up smoking—unless you really want to, you won't. And you'll never convince anyone else—like your spouse—to do it either unless they are of the same mind-set.

Ready, Set, Go

Once you've made up your mind to start exercising, begin by consulting your physician, especially if you haven't exercised for a long time, or have any chronic health problems or concerns. After you get the green light, take it slowly. For advice on how to best begin, I turned to the wonderful Christine King, renowned fitness expert and medical exercise specialist, also known as South Florida's "First Lady of Fitness."

"Many go into their exercise program doing too much too fast. This is a mistake as it leads to over-soreness, fatigue, and injury. (As we just saw with Lorraine!) Keep in mind that your body didn't end up this way overnight and that the cure doesn't happen overnight, either!" So Christine suggests that we take time and enjoy the changes we will inevitably see and feel in the short-term after we first make a commitment. "If you stick to a moderate program, the positive results will motivate you to stay with it." Furthermore, "you must have a concrete plan, preferably written, and then it must be implemented into your daily schedule. Please remember that you're making promises to yourself, no one else. You are the one who needs to look in the mirror each morning and either feel great about your accomplishments or disappointed for not following through."

It Makes Sense(s)

It's a good idea to use what we learned in Rung 2—Emotional Well-Being and engage all our senses to give us a jump-start. "Take the visual," says Dan Nguyen, an L.A.-based certified trainer and fitness behavior expert. "Just find a picture of someone who has the abs, let's say, that you want, and visualize yourself floating into that picture. Now imagine what it feels like to be that person."

Then comes auditory: "What does it sound like once you reach your goal? Maybe you hear friends and family giving you compliments." Finally, there's sensory: "What does your body feel like when you accomplish that goal? How will you stand? How will you breathe?"

Above all, it is counterproductive to set unreasonable and unreachable goals. We must work toward achieving our goal of optimal fitness slowly, taking baby steps. Just resolve to include one physical activity you love in your day to get your blood flowing and exercise your muscles, heart, and lungs. If you work in an office, make a point of getting up to talk to a colleague by walking to his or her office, rather than communicating through an e-mail or a phone call. Sit and stand up from your chair 30 times every hour or two. When shopping, go first for a brisk walk around the block or the mall. Then walk a little faster and a little longer. As you progress and you're successful with the first changes, you can make another one after a month or so. For instance, begin alternating your walking with short bursts of jogging.

Once you're ready to take the next step, it is time to build up a more complete exercise program, one that expands your newfound or improved cardiovascular fitness level to include your whole body. That's when you need to avoid Lorraine's mistake! If you decide to go to a gym (small, medium, or mega), have a one-hour consultation with an on-staff trainer who will assess your fitness level and develop a personalized exercise program.

We each have our own reasons for wanting to exercise. My friend Judy claims she has an hourglass figure. Only now, due to age and the birth of multiple offspring, all the sand has sunk to the bottom, making the shape more like a pear. (Trust me, she is not alone in this complaint!) A neighbor of mine said that she glanced into a mirror in a fitting room that showed what she looked like from the back in a bathing suit. "Jane," she lamented, "I said to myself, what is that thing around my thighs? I knew I had to start working out when I realized with horror that it was, in fact, my behind."

Whatever your incentive to get started, the time is now! For those who aren't already exercise experienced, let's keep in mind the ancient Chinese proverb: A voyage of 1,000 miles begins with the first step—or in our case, steps.

Walking 101

Walking is a simple and effective way to exercise, as it requires no special equipment or training. Even if your exercise regimen centers on swimming or spinning, you should also make concentrated walking part of your day. And if aches, pains, or injuries (and who doesn't have an assortment of those?) prevent you from doing anything too extreme, walking by itself can be a surprisingly effective weight control tool if you do it regularly. I personally love to walk. However, I've often wondered if I'm actually going about it the right way. According to Jonathan FitzGordon, fitness author and founder of the CoreWalking Program, the way we walk often causes long-term damage to our bodies.

"Most people walk in a way that makes their chronic pain and injury worse because of their often harmful, deeply ingrained movement patterns. And since walking is a habitual activity we do more than almost any other, for those who aren't suffering discomfort now, the future sadly often holds this fate."

His program's philosophy rests on the belief in our ability to change and evolve as we age. In fact, he insists that you're never too old, or too young, to learn to break bad habits. And almost anyone can alleviate pain and improve his/her physical health and life. FitzGordon contends that while the majority of back and hip pain we experience may not necessarily be created by our walking and standing patterns, it is most definitely exacerbated by them. On the other hand, if we learn to walk and stand correctly, the body actually works more efficiently and effectively, which frees us up for healing.

"The first thing you can do to make a change is a little self-analysis. For instance, how do you wear out your shoes?" Apparently, most people are wearing them out on the outside of the foot when it should be the inside of the front of the foot that wears most.

"If you are ready to move, stick your butt out, lean slightly forward, and start walking. Walking is literally falling, and you have to learn to let the body catch itself." Here are seven more quick steps:

- Don't lean backward to walk forward.
- Don't hyperextend your knees when walking, instead leave them gently relaxed.
- Untuck your pelvis. When you do this, your feet with fall more naturally toward parallel.
- Look straight ahead at a horizon line.
- Take shorter strides.
- Relax your arms so they are free to swing, consciously move arms and legs in opposition to each other.
- Don't hit your heel hard (that is a function of leaning backward). When you start moving forward, use much more of the foot.

Stretch It Out

Once you are ready to go beyond moderate walking on flat surfaces, you will be setting out to engage your muscles, tendons, ligaments, and joints in more challenging ways. But before you do, it is important to learn how to increase their flexibility and elasticity through stretching. Marc Perry explains, "Flexibility is defined as the range of motion within a joint along the various planes of motion. Within each joint, there is an optimal range of motion (ROM) that is crucial for peak performance. Stretching refers to the process of elongating the muscles to improve ROM. Static stretching is when you stretch while staying stationary, which is the preferred type of stretching during and after exercise. I think for anyone who can improve ROM, static stretching is very helpful, if not essential."

Here are some of its pluses—increased movement efficiency, decreased risk for injury, and improved blood supply and nutrients to joint structures, increased neuromuscular coordination, decreased risk for low-back pain, reduced muscular tension, and improved balance and postural awareness. Its negatives, if performed properly—not having any of those! Although it is important to remember that stretching can be harmful if overdone or done the wrong way. In other words, if you feel the stretch is causing any pain, beyond that of the mild pulling sensation caused by making your muscles expand out of their contracted comfort zone, STOP!

Go Back in Time

After you've stretched, the next phase in building your exercise regime should be toward a general full-body activity. The best is swimming, since it is 100 percent non-weight bearing on the joints and requires almost every muscle to do it right. But that requires a swimming pool or beach. So before you get caught up in something as specialized as swimming or spinning (or speed dating), take a page from your gym class at school.

"Think back to the calisthenics from phys ed class," says Kim Watters, fitness manager at Red Mountain Resort in St. George, Utah. "It turns out that P.E. teachers were on the right track. Full-body exercises such as jumping jacks and push-ups are more effective and don't require fancy gym equipment. I tell guests that the only thing they need is their body." Watters says there are several full-body moves that can be combined to maximize results, including sprints, jumping jacks, squats, lunges, and push-ups. Here is Watters's favorite at-home workout for getting into shape:

1. Warm up with a one-mile jog or run
2. Do 25 jumping jacks
3. Step back into 20 alternating lunges
4. Do 12 push-ups, then transition with a forward roll or side roll into sit-ups

5. Do as many sit-ups as possible in two minutes (Note: for those with back pain, replace sit-ups with curl-ups or crunches on a stability ball.)

Fitness Should Be Fun

Okay, calisthenics aren't for everyone. Thankfully, there are other options to make exercise fun. And trial and error isn't bad to find what motivates you and keeps you from getting bored. In fact, that is the whole theory behind integrated facilities that combine all the usual exercise equipment and classes, with indoor and outdoor tennis courts and Olympic swimming pools, plus squash courts, basketball courts, kids' academies, karate schools, beauty salons, and restaurants.

But you don't have to go supersize to find what works best for you. Far and away the greatest growth area in the fitness world is still at the other end of the spectrum—small standalone studios, either local or part of a large national chain. So go big, go small, or go in-between, just look for your physical and psychological comfort zone.

Another point to keep in mind is that our bodies are designed to have complementary muscles—think biceps and triceps. That is also true for different parts of the same system, like calves and thighs. Repetitive use of only one (or a few) set(s), can lead to a variety of structural issues. So if you do patronize a specialty studio or gym, either supplement your in-studio workouts with at-home or outdoor exercises, or rotate your studios.

No Pain, No Gain?

When working out, it's important to differentiate between discomfort and pain. True pain is the body's signal that it is—or is about to be—injured and should be immediately respected. But some pain for better gain has just received a scientific boost! Fitness experts have talked for years about making your muscles bigger through "micro-tears" resulting from pushing yourself beyond prior levels. This explains the "burn" you feel, which is really a build-up of lactic acid.

Now, a recent study by Scripps Research Institute in Florida has shown that the chemicals the body produces in the adrenaline class (called catecholamines), designed to help us in the "fight or flight" response, actually work at a cellular level to increase muscle growth and fitness. The catch is that we have to feel under duress to do so. Researchers found that intense exercise fools the body into thinking it is under attack—and bingo!—catecholamines. However, doing the same intense exercise repeatedly will eventually educate your body to the fact that that particular activity is non-threatening, so it stops making the magic bullets. That's another reason to alternate your exercise regimes.

Run for It

Perhaps the most popular form of strenuous exercise is jogging and running, even though the practitioners never seem to be smiling. I have to admit that even before I had a steel rod and plate in my left ankle and a ceramic right hip, I never found running for anything other than the phone appealing. But millions do. And long-distance running goes way back. In 490 BC, Pheidippides ran the 26 miles and 385 yards to Athens from Marathon (ergo the name), then delivered the momentous message "Niki!" ("Victory!"). Alas, he then promptly collapsed and died. So it obviously wasn't great for *his* health. But that was then and this is now!

According to the latest research conducted by Paul Williams at the Berkeley Lab's Life Sciences Division, running longer distances actually decreases a person's risk for osteoarthritis and hip replacements. Williams's results counter the common belief that the constant pounding (what the fitness folk call "high impact") of running breaks down the cartilage that protects our knees and leads to osteoarthritis.

In fact, those who ran more than 1.2 miles per day were at 15 percent less risk for osteoarthritis and 35 percent less risk for hip replacements than more sedentary men and women.

These risks did not increase at higher mileages, even in runners who logged multiple marathons per year. Further analyses revealed that running reduced the risk for these injuries due, in part, to the sport's association with lower body mass index.

"It is important to understand the remarkable machine our body is," Williams states. "We think of machines as wearing out over time. The durability of a machine is not improved by using it more. The body, though, is different. It tends to divert its resources depending upon need, strengthening those parts that get the greatest use." In the case of running, the standard "machine scenario" suggests that the joints will eventually wear out, where more and more scientific research shows that the body responds by "thickening cartilage and increasing glycosaminoglycans, the chemicals used by the body to synthesize proteoglycans, which provides the cartilage's viscoelastic properties." (While I may not be able to pronounce it, I get the point: Running helps the body's flexibility and its production of shock absorbers.)

Williams also found that people who engaged in non-running and non-walking exercises that put stress on the joints had increased rates of osteoarthritis and hip replacements. "Osteoarthritis has been reported to increase in soccer players and weight lifters, and in occupations requiring knee-bends, kneeling, or squats, which may be more characteristic of exercises performed in gyms, circuit training, and aerobic classes."

Of course, one way that running lowers the risk for osteoarthritis and hip replacement is by keeping people lean. Being overweight is a well-known risk factor for these conditions. "Running helps prevent age-related weight gain and helps us regulate our calorie intake better."

But don't start out running a marathon, or even a 5K (I was sore for a week just from trying to *speed-walk* my first 5K). Joan Benoit Samuelson, the greatest American woman runner of all time and winner of the very first Olympic gold medal for a women's marathon, advises for running neophytes: "Even doing measured running, for example, running from one telephone pole to another if you are on a country road, or one house to the next, will start you on the right track. Or do ten steps walking, then ten running, then twenty steps walking and then running, until you reach a hundred of each."

The National Runners' and Walkers' studies have revealed a number of remarkable health benefits from exercise in general. It decreases the risk for stroke by 69 percent, heart disease by 37 percent, benign prostate enlargement by 33 percent, gout by 45 percent, gallbladder disease by 52 percent, diverticular disease by 48 percent, cataracts by 35 percent, age-related macular degeneration by 54 percent, glaucoma by 43 percent, high blood pressure by 30 percent, high cholesterol by 47 percent, and diabetes by 68 percent There are no other drugs or genetic discoveries that come close to producing these health values.

Be a Sport

Full-court basketball, soccer, competitive rowing, and cycling are just some of the many sports that require a high degree of conditioning and, in return, provide a great deal of exercise. Just remember that it doesn't have to be a martial art or tackle football to hurt! What most team sports have in common is sudden starts, stops, and turns—due in part to the fact that you are not always (or ever) in full control of what is going on about you.

It is nice to see that nowadays even professional athletes make sure to go through stretching routines before games. So the bottom line is that regularly participating in sports is probably the most enjoyable form of exercise, but only if you don't have to leave the game with a torn hamstring or sprained ankle!

To avoid any sprains or strains, a sport that is getting a lot of attention is scuba diving. It wouldn't normally have been my first choice—or any choice, for that matter. The reason being that one summer, when my brother and I were kids, he playfully (I hope) held my head under the water when we were in the ocean. I thought I was going to drown. So you can just imagine how I might feel about deep-sea diving. I mean, one rarely goes back to crime scenes unless you're Ted Danson on *CSI*. However, when a press release came across my desk recently, talking about improving our well-being through scuba diving, I must admit that I was intrigued.

"Because diving is a low-impact sport, many divers do not and should not feel the physical exertion underwater; but they are, in fact, using major muscle groups to propel themselves through resistance created by the water," says Kelly Rockwood, PADI (Professional Association of Diving Instructors) Americas course director. "It's a great workout for anybody, simply because you are, for the most part, in a very low-impact environment. And it's also balanced because it involves not only your leg muscles, but it's cardio, too." To that end, many specialists have also suggested diving as a supplement to athletes' running, biking, and other sports' activity, as being in the water can strengthen different muscle groups and help prevent injury.

It doesn't have to be scuba diving, of course. Just pick any sport you like. If you find one that you enjoy, you'll make it a regular part of your fitness regimen, whether at home or on vacation. And that's really what exercise should be all about.

Wish Upon a Spa

I was extremely fortunate to have a mother who was a true pioneer in trying and writing about fitness resorts in the United States, a passion I inherited and followed both writing for the *International Herald Tribune* when we lived in Paris many years ago and back home at *Town & Country* magazine for well over a decade. What I (and The Lawyer) learned beyond doubt is that there is absolutely no better way to launch into a fitness program than starting it out under the 24/7 guidance of a good spa. The word *spa* in fact comes from the name of the resort town in southern Belgium that was an early health (meaning, taking the water cure) stop favored by the likes of Peter the Great. (Yes, *that* Peter the Great!).

Our American version is devoted to exercise, though, and was founded by Deborah Szekely in the late 1940s, ironically, across the border in Tecate, Mexico, at Rancho La Puerta. "The Ranch," which is still there and thriving (along with its upscale younger sister, The Golden Door, in Escondido, California), broke the mold of the "fat farm" that catered only to the obese and was based almost entirely on drastic diets. Its progeny are everywhere today, offering all kinds of workout plans and attracting both the young and fit, along with those just getting started.

Today, this American-style destination spa can be found all over the country, and they provide an amazing palette of traditional and innovative exercise programs, as well as nutritionally oriented diet regimens and experts to help you achieve your goals. The choices are enormous. There are the super spas, which offer luxurious accommodations, provide a plethora of fitness resources and classes, and tend to have delicious yet healthy and nutritious meals. There are also specialty spas that focus on one or just a few types of regimens—it could be anything from specific exercise programs to specialty diets such as vegan. If you need direction, click onto or contact SpaFinders.com, tell them what you want out of your spa experience, preferred location (anywhere in the world), and your price range, and let them guide you.

The ones I find most interesting are the "Ashrams" that provide skillful advice and leadership in yoga. Sadly, ever since The Lawyer got stuck in a pretzel position while doing a pose, he was never again willing to join me for yoga. A currently hot (literally!) form is, in fact, hot yoga, which is done in a room heated to Guam-like climate. If that seems a bit much, start off by trying a spa (or local studio) devoted to the gentle stretches of Hatha yoga, which is known for its breathing exercises.

Take It on Home

Going to a secluded spa of any kind is not for, or affordable by, everyone. And while they are great for starting or developing a fitness regime, you can also bring some of the spa experience home with you. Dr. Carmella Sebastian, author of *Sex and Spaghetti Sauce*, says that even cleaning your house can be wonderful exercise. For example, standing at the sink doing dishes gives you the chance to do deep knee bends. Vacuuming the house from top to bottom can be as good as aerobics. If your washer and dryer are downstairs in the basement, several trips up and down those steps can be good cardio. In fact, she advises that a full cleaning spree can burn almost 200 calories an hour!

You don't need an expensive gym or piles of equipment. What you do need is a degree of focus and commitment. For example, don't try to find a parking space right by where you're going. Pull into the first space and walk the rest of the way. "Okay, it's a cliché, but stop passing the staircase in favor of the elevator. Pull out your weed whacker or mower and rev it up yourself instead of paying the teenager next door to do it for you. Take walking breaks instead of coffee breaks. If you incorporate extra steps and extra movement into whatever you do, you'll find those steps may add up to a half an hour or more of extra exercise each day. Remember, staying fit is about staying moving."

She suggests that you start with 30 minutes of walking, three times a week, and build up from 30 to 60 minutes at a time, three times a week. If you have time and energy to walk more often or more frequently, that's even better. And finally, let your walks double as bonding time. You're much more likely to keep up healthy habits if someone is holding you accountable. So grab a friend, partner, neighbor, or even your pet when you head out for a walk.

Commit to Being Fit

According to the University of Scranton, statistics indicate that those who explicitly commit to being fit are 10 times more likely to attain their goals than people who do not. Create a plan. Write down your goals. Make a promise to yourself that you'll do even one activity a day to make you Fitter Than Before!

Putting It All Together

The best way to keep track of your fitness goals is to chronicle what type of exercise you are doing and how much time you are devoting to it. One study confirms that simply looking through your journal—even if you have just walked for 10 minutes—will inspire you to do more exercise on a regular basis.

Now here's how to incorporate exercise into all nine rungs, courtesy of Christine King:

1. *Doctor's Orders*—Always speak to your doctor prior to beginning any exercise program to find out if there are specific guidelines relating to your existing health conditions.

2. *Emotional Well-Being*—Beginning an exercise program or enhancing an existing one will markedly improve your emotional health. Physical activity increases your level of endorphins, which resemble opiates in their abilities to produce analgesia and a feeling of well-being.

3. *Nutrition*—In order for you to feel good and have the energy to make it through your day and exercise program, your body needs fuel. That means proper nutrition.

4. *Fitness*—See above!

5. *Beauty*—Being healthy and fit naturally shrouds you with a beautiful glow. It increases blood flow, which improves your color and also gives you the undeniable internal beauty that is immeasurable. You'll feel vibrant, beautiful, and sexy.

6. *Natural Remedies*—Exercise is the only true fountain of youth. It is the natural cure and prevention of most diseases and ailments. People who exercise are healthier, happier, have elevated immune systems, and recover from ailments faster.

7. *Spirituality*—Many modalities of fitness include the element of spirituality. Yoga, Pilates, martial arts, and infusing the art of meditation and breathing complete the circle in any element of movement.

8. *Support*—There is no better key to success in fitness than support from a buddy. Grab a friend and be accountable to each other to hit the gym on your scheduled days. Your success will improve tenfold.

9. *Giving Back*—Taking care of yourself allows you to give back to your family in more ways than one. If a family member really needs you, how can you expect to help if you're not well yourself? You also become a role model as everyone notices the transformation while you journey through the rungs, and it will inspire them to join you on your climb.

So before you consider trying to change your life around by consulting a life coach, psychic, divorce lawyer, or a matchmaker, start by putting on your sneakers and getting your patootie in gear!

Key Concepts from
Rung 4—Fitness

Concept _____

Why It Interests Me _____

_____

_____

_____

_____

How could I apply it to my life? _____

_____

_____

_____

_____

Concept _____

Why It Interests Me _____

_____

_____

_____

_____

How could I apply it to my life? _____

_____

_____

_____

_____

Concepts to Share

Concept _____
_____
_____
_____

With Whom? _____
_____
_____
_____

Concept _____
_____
_____
_____

With Whom? _____
_____
_____
_____

Concept _____
_____
_____
_____

With Whom? _____
_____
_____
_____

Beauty

"Nothing makes a woman more beautiful than the belief that she is beautiful."

—Sophia Loren

Look Good to Feel Better

My mother, Emily, was one of the world's great beauties. So much so that Estée Lauder, her close friend, followed her to Havana on her honeymoon to test her sun creams on her flawless complexion. Of course, it's never easy being the daughter of somebody that gorgeous. "Jane would be beautiful if she just combed her hair," I remember her telling others when I was a teenager. (Thanks, Mom!) But she also told me, "Take good care of yourself, sweetheart, 'cause you are the only self you have!" Needless to say, her advice was always correct and way ahead of its time. And her knowledge of all things beauty became my legacy as well.

Aside from writing the first-ever books on spas, Emily wrote two more pioneering primers on beauty and grooming. "Every girl has the potential for beauty," she believed. And as a founder and member of the Board of Trustees of the prestigious Fashion Institute of Technology in New York City, she created the Emily Wilkens Chair in External Impressions to help students, as she said at the time, "find new beauty, contentment, health, and confidence about who they are and what they looked like." She also believed that a happy person has a glow to her skin that was undeniable. And that a lack of enthusiasm for life wrinkles your soul.

This program was the precursor to today's concept of the makeover. I still recall being amazed by the before- and after-photos she brought home. In her workshop, she simplified the process of self-improvement. Point by point, she corrected misconceptions about grooming (a word used in those times), solved seemingly unsolvable problems, and turned negative attitudes into positive ones. Just by standing up straighter, changing hair and makeup, and having a heightened sense of self-esteem, her students' physical appearance improved noticeably.

"Beauty is also an attitude," she would say. "Yes, life happens. But it doesn't have to show on your skin. And you are only as beautiful as you think you are. When you walk into a room, hold your head up high. The secret is to visualize yourself as the most important person in the entire place, the person that everyone else wants to see—and be! If you imagine it vividly enough, you will become that person." Above all, she emphasized that everyone should work on inner beauty, and that didn't cost a thing. "Smile," she would say, "take a brisk walk, read to enrich your mind, and relax! Worry, like stress, drains beauty!"

The effectiveness of this concept was further brought to light for me when I was writing the "Beauty Talk" column for *Town & Country* magazine. During that time, I became involved with a cosmetic and fragrance industry initiative called "Look Good Feel Better" that helped women cancer patients improve their appearance and self-image by teaching them hands-on beauty techniques. The very valid assumption was that when survivors were able to see themselves in a more positive light, the healing process would get a big boost.

That's why the Beauty Rung is right in the middle of our Ladder. Being Better Than Before doesn't start with beauty or end with it; but since so much of our self-esteem revolves around how we see ourselves and how others see us, our Ladder, like our lives, does have beauty at its center. (And not just for women, as industry statistics show the biggest growth area in personal care is in men's products!) Beauty is not an absolute. It also isn't the same for everyone or for anyone at every age. So we go back to the original Kaizen concept—improvement through small, incremental change at any age.

Skin-Deep Beauty

Like my mother, I absolutely reject the idea that beauty is only skin deep. At its most essential, beauty comes from the aura we project from inside, from self-assurance, while health and fitness give us our glow. But that is not to say that our skin doesn't play a critical role in our being more beautiful inside and out. And we're not just talking about our complexions!

Good skin care starts with the same rule as the maxim of doctors: First do no harm! When it comes to damaging your skin, the chief villains are no surprise—the big three Ss—Sun, Smoking, and Stress, plus poor nutrition, too little water, too much alcohol, and not enough sleep.

The ABCs of Ultraviolet Rays (UVR)

Don't think that just because you can't see the sun that you're safe; sun damage can occur even on cloudy days. In fact, ultraviolet rays easily penetrate the atmosphere under any weather condition. Happily, a recent study published in the *Annals of Internal Medicine* shows sunscreen may prevent skin aging and possibly help reverse it.

UV rays come in two basic variations—UVA and UVB. (Think UVA for aging and UVB for burning.) Wrinkles, sagging, leathering, and discoloration are all UVR-related. Worse, each year more than 3.5 million cases of skin cancer are diagnosed in the United States, more than 90 percent of which are caused by the sun. And the damage is cumulative. Fortunately, the vast majority of skin cancers are basal cell carcinomas and squamous cells carcinomas. While malignant, meaning that they can invade and destroy nearby tissue, these are unlikely to metastasize, meaning to spread to other parts of the body.

Dr. Susan Stuart, a board-certified La Jolla dermatologist, contends that a tan is never safe, whether you acquire it on the beach or in a salon. "Although tanning salon operators may say their new bulbs are safe and that some UV exposure is necessary for vitamin D, neither statement is true." In fact, people who use tanning beds are 2.5 times more likely to develop squamous cell carcinoma and 1.5 times more likely to develop basal cell carcinoma. Worst of all, even occasional sunbed use almost triples your chances of developing melanoma, the type of skin cancer than can metastasize.

According to the doctor, the new high-pressure sunlamps actually emit UVR doses as much as 12 times that of the sun. When unprotected skin is overexposed to UVR, DNA is damaged; a tan is the skin's attempt to prevent further damage by creating a wall of darker pigment. And damage that has already occurred can lead to changes (mutations) in skin cell DNA. "In general, it is far better to obtain vitamin D through D-rich foods, such as salmon, fortified milk or orange juice, and/or dietary supplements."

So whenever you venture out in the sun, be smart about it by following Dr. Stuart's seven simple rules:

- Seek the shade whenever possible, especially between 10 AM and 4 PM.
- Don't burn. When you see your skin redden, take cover.
- Avoid tanning and UV booths.
- Use a broad-spectrum (UVA/UVB) sunscreen with an SPF of 15 or higher every day.
- Cover up with clothing, including a broad-brimmed hat and UVR-blocking sunglasses.
- Be sure to protect your kids, too. Just one severe burn in childhood doubles the chances of developing melanoma later in life.
- After two hours in the sun, sunscreen loses effectiveness, so it's vital to reapply. Furthermore, no sunscreen is com-

pletely waterproof, so if you've been swimming or exercising heavily, reapply immediately.

Finally, besides looking for sunscreens that offer broad-spectrum or UVA/UVB protection, make sure they have one or more UVA-filtering ingredients such as titanium dioxide or zinc oxide. And use them every day, in every kind of weather. Also, wear proper sunglasses whenever it's bright or glary. Besides the obvious benefit of protecting your eyes, prolonged squinting can lead to the wrinkling around the eyes that we know as the dreaded crow's feet.

Fear Factor

Now, I know I've been telling you all along that worrying can be harmful to your health. But University of Buffalo researchers say that when it comes to preventing skin cancer, a little fear is good for you. In a study published in the *Journal of Behavioral Medicine*, the researchers found that worrying about skin cancer had a bigger influence on people's use of sunscreen than information about the statistical likelihood of developing the disease.

According to the Centers for Disease Control and Prevention, skin cancer is the most common form of cancer in the United States. In 2011 alone, more than 70,000 people were diagnosed with the worst kind of skin cancer, malignant melanomas, with over 12,000 people dying from them. Furthermore, malignant melanoma is the number-one cause of death from cancer in women in their 20s to 30s. Three key actions can help make sun exposure safer: Prevent, detect, and treat skin cancer as early as possible. Education is key, as well as acceptance. Many patients avoid having their skin screened or treated due to fear or embarrassment. But as I say to my kids who honestly believe that their parents sole mission in life is to mortify their children, "Get over it."

The ABCDs of Moles and Melanoma

Most people have some skin marks, such as freckles, moles, or birthmarks. Go to a dermatologist once a year and have them checked out. Here are the ABCDs of Moles and Melanoma, according to board-certified dermatologist Dr. Steven Rotter:

- *Asymmetry*: Melanomas are usually characterized by an irregular, asymmetrical shape. This means that one half of the spot does not match the other half.
- *Border*: The edges of the old mole may turn scalloped or rough. New skin spots with undefined borders may also appear.
- *Color*: Existing or new fast-growing moles with uneven coloring (various shades of brown or black, colorless areas) are the first signs of skin cancer. These spots may later become red, blue, or white.
- *Diameter*: Early melanoma spots usually are greater than six millimeters in diameter.

Dr. Rotter also suggests looking for any changes in a mole, including the following possible signs:

- You may notice that new spots or existing skin moles start to grow fast.
- Melanomas come in a variety of colors. An early sign of skin cancer is the color distribution; color spreads from the borders of the mole into the surrounding skin area.
- Moles that are usually flat begin to grow vertically.
- Inflammation occurs on the surrounding area of a new pigmented skin formation.
- Melanoma formation is characterized by the change in the surface of a mole, including an erosion, oozing, scaliness, and even bleeding.
- The most common sign of skin cancer is an itching sensation in the infected areas. Skin cancers are usually painless, but some people with melanomas may experience a little pain and tenderness.

Stop Smoking

Let me be frank: smoking is wrong on every level! I always tell smokers just to take a walk through the lung cancer floor at any cancer hospital. They'll think twice about ever picking up another cigarette. But skin-wise, at the very least, repeated squinting to avoid the draft and the pursing of a smoker's lips to draw on the cigarette (or cigar) lead to wrinkling around the eyes and mouth. More importantly, smoking produces compounds in your tissues and in your bloodstream that produce free radicals, which are the oxygen-related compounds that create damage. Therefore, smoking accelerates the decay and breakdown of the epidermis (the outermost layers of skin cells). And of course, the harm it does to pretty much all your other organs will result in damage to your skin, as well!

De-Stress

As we've talked about in previous rungs, stress is bad for your health. Period. In fact, The Lawyer says my nagging about, say, his diet will give him a heart attack faster than a deep-dish pizza. (Nice try!) Stress causes the skin to be deprived of nutrients, which eventually affects its appearance. You can always tell if a person is going through a traumatic event because it has a tremendous impact on the way they look. They can appear to age years in just a short period of time.

And then there are the worry lines. Frowning, turning your lips down, pinching your forehead, and even "wrinkling your brow" all cause wrinkles. On the other hand, smiling is a great facial exercise that gives many of our 43 facial muscles a good workout.

Above all, however, no amount of makeup, creams, lotions, potions, or injections is going to make you feel attractive if you are unhappy. Anxiety (fear) is the primary contributing factor to looking old and unattractive. It can drive us to destructive behaviors—too much sun, smoking, drinking alcohol, eating the wrong food, sleeplessness, and so on. If stress is the number one factor in diminishing your healthy, beautiful look, then it makes sense that feeling good contributes to your beauty in a positive way.

From the Inside Out

As we talked about in Rung 3—Nutrition, the best diet, and one that benefits the skin, too, includes high-impact, low-inflammatory, antioxidant-rich foods such as whole grains, leafy greens (all vegetables for that matter), and lean proteins. In fact, since your skin is protein-based, anything that helps these protein-based layers stay healthy will make your skin better; and conversely, anything that hurts them will make your skin dry and cracked, and therefore wrinkled. So go easy on the salt, white sugar, processed foods, and saturated fats. Good fats for the skin are the omega-3 essential fatty acids.

What's more important than protein for your skin? Water! Like the rest of our body, our skin is mostly H_2O. But unlike our insides, our skin is exposed to the outside air, meaning that evaporation constantly dries it out. We add water topically through moisturizers, and try to retain it with products containing humectants. But nothing is as beneficial as replacing water the old-fashioned way—by drinking it. A classic mistake is not hydrating enough because you're not thirsty. Drinking eight glasses of water a day is the basic rule for healthy skin (just like for all our other organs).

No Cheers Here

Unlike water, alcohol is dehydrating. Not surprisingly, then, the biggest issue with drinking alcohol is dehydration. If you dehydrate your body, you are going to indirectly dehydrate your skin, which leads to lines and wrinkles.

Broken capillaries on the face or nose are much more commonly caused by accumulated sun exposure than by alcohol. (Maybe W.C. Fields was simply a sun worshipper.) Facial or body flushing, though, can be associated with excessive alcohol production and is caused by accumulation of alcohol byproducts in the blood.

Alcohol is also a depressant. It can cause you to think more slowly and have less energy. It can also cause tired skin! So the net-net is that when you look tired, you're not going to look as good.

Ready ... Set ... Glow

Alas, while we may be able to control factors such as sun exposure, smoking, stress, and nutrition, we cannot stop the aging process. In theory, age is something that shouldn't matter—unless you're a cheddar cheese. But clearly, we do live in a very youth-oriented society, which is why the beauty industry, especially the segment devoted to "anti-aging" products, is growing at such at rapid rate. Every day there seems to be a new skin-care product, service, or "expert" shedding light on how our daily activities affect our complexion—and how we can slow the effects of aging.

Over the years, I have always been an intrepid sleuth, and I would never let a possible beauty secret escape my watch. But the one bit of advice that has always resonated with me was something that Estée Lauder once told me: "Jane, your face is the first thing that people see. Take good care of it." At the end of the day, no amount of plastic surgery or any cosmetic procedure will make you look any younger if your skin isn't good to begin with, which requires care from the inside out.

> Your skin is made up mostly of the proteins collagen, elastin, and keratin. Its structure is complex, but the skin is the only tissue in the body designed to both block out harmful irritants, pathogens, and radiation, while releasing perspiration and toxins through our pores. So, keeping the surface healthy and the pores open are critical.

Glisten Up

When it comes to putting your best face forward, let me start by answering the most common questions that both my readers and listeners have asked over the years.

1. Will my face age just like my mom's?

(Funny, I've never received this question from a man about his father's skin.)

If your mother's skin didn't age well, that doesn't mean yours won't! Genetics does play a role in how your skin looks, from the size of your pores to its texture and color. But banking on aging like your mom or grandmother is a big mistake. Being unhealthy can make more of a difference than what you inherit. Also, the environment, exposing your skin to the sun, and availability of skincare products and treatments make any meaningful comparison generation to generation impossible.

2. Is it okay to drink coffee?

Skin-wise, there are very few, if any, studies that have focused on any damage from, or cosmetic benefits of, caffeine consumption specifically. The good news is that a Harvard study reported that caffeine consumption was associated with a reduced risk of basal cell carcinoma of the skin. Just remember that caffeine is a diuretic, and as we've learned, dehydration is a major enemy of our skin.

3. Should I really cleanse my face every night before bed?

Yes, you should! Sleeping with makeup on will leave your skin's pores clogged and prevent it from breathing.

4. Is stronger always more effective?

No! Using harsh cleansers will strip away the natural oils that protect your face from dirt, pollution, and other factors that can easily damage your skin. Do your face a favor and use mild cleansers. Again, moisture is key. Strong cleansers also dry the surface of your skin and strip away the protective layer that retains moisture. This is particularly true of prescription-strength skin peeling products. Use them only with a dermatologist's, or at least a well-qualified cosmetologist's, advice!

5. Are eye creams important for my beauty regimen, or are they just hype?

The area around your eyes is the most delicate part of your face and where fine lines will appear first, so having a specialized eye cream, rather than your usual moisturizer, is strongly suggested, normally after age 25.

6. *When it comes to my face, is more always better?*

More is almost always worse. In other words, too much washing, too much cream, too much scrub can cause more harm than good. Not to mention too much smoking (which is any!), too much alcohol, too much sun, and too many fatty foods!

7. *I have the same kinds of complexion problems as my teen-ager—at age 50?*

This is not all that uncommon. Adult acne tends to be concentrated on the lower half of the face, especially around the chin and jawline. It can include whiteheads, blackheads, pimples, and deeper cysts and nodules. Hormonal changes related to your period, pregnancy, perimenopause, and menopause can trigger or aggravate acne, as well as stress and the use of certain medications (e.g., oral contraceptives, corticosteroids, or lithium). It is important to recognize that aging skin is also drier; so in this case, too, less can be more. Over-the-counter creams, gels, or lotions that contain higher percentages of benzoyl peroxide may irritate and dry out your skin. Instead, opt for a prescription treatment containing retinoids, which work by unplugging clogged pores.

8. *What can I do to look younger?*

This is probably the question I am asked most of all. Alas, we are an age-obsessed country. And it's truer in America than anywhere else. In Europe, for example, age really doesn't seem to matter nearly as much. Women are admired for their beauty, sensuality, and intelligence, not their youth. Aside from taking good care of yourself, know that the essence of youth is glow. And it's the loss of glow that makes us look older at any age. Everyone needs help. The older we get the more we need. You just have to add more glow with make-up and moisturizers. That's all there is to it. And don't get too thin, which always makes your face look older. There comes a time in life to choose between your face and your hips.

Read Between the Lines

Aside from the questions above, the subject on many women's (and again, increasingly men's) minds is cosmetic surgery. Until as recently as a decade ago, the only available medical antidote for aging skin involved scalpels, anesthesia, and long and painful recoveries. For some, that meant faces that were pulled and stretched so taut that the results were, well, scary. We've all seen them. These are the people who will smile through any problem—not because they have achieved Nirvana, but because they simply physically cannot frown.

But going under the knife isn't always the answer. Fortunately, there are now many effective, noninvasive treatments and techniques, which, along with a holistic approach to taking good care of yourself, will leave you looking and feeling not a day over fabulous, no matter what your actual age.

According to Dr. Haideh Hirmand, a leading Harvard-educated New York City plastic surgeon, the goal is to look flawless while still letting your unique beauty shine through.

"It's important to distinguish between the 'wanting to look young' look, which implies age, from the 'looking naturally youthful at any age' appearance, which implies youth. Fortunately, today we can actually change the direction of aging. Studies have shown that fillers can create new collagen, and neuromodulators (like Botox) redirect the way we move our faces. So you can slow down the genetic aging pattern that your skin will pursue."

So when is the right time to have cosmetic surgery? "I would say only when you are psychologically and practically ready for it. It's a personal decision and a big step, but sometimes it's the only sure way to get a great result."

Of course, until we come to the decision—or if, like me, you are terrified of anything that even remotely relates to an operating room—there are many other options available today. Fillers and energy devices, such as micro-focused ultrasound and lasers, can help postpone the need for something more drastic.

Dr. Hirmand cautions, however, that you should never have any cosmetic medical treatments done in a nonmedical setting. (I saw an announcement the other day for a mani/pedi/ Botox special in the local nail salon! Seriously?) A great deal of distortion can be done with fillers if used incorrectly, disproportionately, or to an extreme, trying to correct a surgical issue. And the "filled" look is just as bad, if not worse, than the "pulled" look of the past!

Also, don't believe the hype about a quick surgical fix. For example, a 15-minute facelift or nose job? Do we really want our surgeons to be going for speed records, like a chef at Benihana's? Dr. Hirmand warns that if it seems too good to be true, it probably is! Be suspicious of catchy marketing names that are not real techniques. "Ask what the procedure actually entails and who is doing it." She also stresses that it is important that all cosmetic procedures be done by a core aesthetic physician. Many doctors call themselves plastic surgeons or facial surgeons, but they may not be properly trained in one of these specialties; so it's important to check if they are board certified and didn't just take a few weekend courses!

Glow and Behold

Rung 4—Fitness showed how important exercise is for our well-being and appearance. We work out our abs, arms, and legs, so why not our faces? After all, there are 43 known muscles around the eyes, across the forehead, along the cheeks, under the mouth, and above the mouth leading down to the chin. And it takes five of them just to display happiness, sadness, fear, anger, disgust, and surprise. Not surprisingly, muscles here are just like muscles everywhere else, they can be made stronger, and doing so firms and tightens the skin around them.

Facial exercises go way back. Some claim Cleopatra started the trend. I can't prove that, but we do know that in 1907 Sanford Bennett published a book called *Exercising in Bed* to reveal "the secret of health, strength, elasticity of body and longevity of life, through a full regime of exercises, including several for the face." Apparently, after two decades of doing said exercises, Mr. Bennett became a veritable Benjamin Button as he grew younger, until at age 70 he had skin that was as smooth as a baby's bottom.

Taking this to the present day, I talked to Sadie Nardini, founder of Core Strength Vinyasa Yoga. "Facial muscles respond to nonuse just like the rest of us—getting saggy over time." Sadie goes on to say that yoga provides us with a face-sculpting, anti-aging prescription for the part of us that the world sees most. And her clients love the benefits of face yoga, which she assures us can improve circulation and lift the neck, jawline, cheeks, and eyes.

You can stimulate the collagen in your face by stretching around the lips and mindfully massaging your entire face. In addition, do the following moves every day in the bathroom mirror before you apply your makeup, says Sadie, "and you may soon notice a glowing, less wrinkle-prone, more youthful face looking back at you!"

- *Lion's Pose*—Relieves mouth and jaw puffiness, stimulates wrinkle-busting collagen and elastin: Inhale through your nose. Exhale, stick out your tongue, and open your mouth as wide as possible. Stick your tongue way out and say AHHHHHHH! Roar like a lion. Repeat five times.
- *Kiss and Yell Pose*—Tones the muscles of the face, neck, and eyes for a natural lift. Purse your lips strongly as if about to give a kiss. At the same time, close your eyes tightly. Open your mouth as wide as you can as if you're yelling. At the same time, open your eyes wide. Repeat 10 times.
- *Eye Rolls*—Tone and refresh the entire eye area and relieve tension and puffiness. Roll your eyes in circles for 10 seconds in each direction, seeking the edge of your ability to stretch them all around. Look up for 10 seconds. Look down for 10 seconds. Finish with circles again. Repeat the sequence three times.

Complexion Perfection

Now that you've prepared your face, we can talk about makeup. Since all the pages of this book could be filled with makeup tips, I've narrowed it down to a few of the most important ones on which I rely. Just remember to have a sense of balance. You never want to look overdone. Note: Don't forget to look in the mirror before you leave the house. Before one holiday party, I had so much to do before I left that I rushed out the door. During the dinner, The Lawyer said, "You look funny!" When I got home I discovered that I had only put mascara on one eye. (Thanks, Bob!) Thankfully, my loopy eyed picture didn't appear on Facebook, Instagram, or Twitter tagged: "Guess who drank all the punch!"

To begin with, invest in a good set of brushes. The secret of makeup artists is that they have eight brushes for different parts of the face.

- Take a little time before you get ready for a special event and smooth on a mask. It will shrink your pores and make your skin look radiant.
- It can be confusing to know what shade of foundation works best for your skin tone. However, don't choose one based on whether your complexion is light or dark. It's your undertone—the warm, cool, or neutral hue that shows through and remains consistent no matter how the surface color changes—that counts. Here's a quick tip: Check the veins on the inside of your wrist. If they look blue/purple, you would choose a base that's in the" cool" family; if they appear green you are in the "warm" spectrum. If it's hard to distinguish whether they are blue or green, you would be "neutral." Better yet, visit a cosmetic counter at your local department store and get "color coded." And try before you buy. The best test is to apply a few strokes on your jawline to see if it matches your skin.
- Even if you have oily skin, you can opt for a cream foundation, which gives the best coverage. Just use a damp

sponge to apply. It will pick up the pigment, but not the oil. I use the foundation brush and buff the color into my skin.

- A tip that I learned from Way Bandy, at one time the industry's most acclaimed makeup artist, is to add a few drops of Visine to your foundation to completely take out any redness. (Like it does for your eyes!)
- To help foundation go on smoother and not look cakey, wear a primer under it—or mix it directly into the foundation—especially if you tend to have combination or dry skin.
- Beware of any glittery shimmer. It won't add a glow to your complexion. It will just make it look shiny.
- For blush, the most important thing is to select colors that appear naturally on your skin. Remember, it's not how much you use, but which shades you choose that make you look made-up or natural. The way to find the perfect blusher is to give your cheeks a pinch; the color they turn is the shade to go with.
- If you like to use powder but still want to look dewy, open up a tissue, tap in some loose powder and fold up the four corners to make a little pouch. Use it as you would a powder puff. The tissue sifts the powder so almost nothing comes through—just enough to set make-up and add a little polish.
- You can change the shape of your face by knowing how to shade and highlight it in the right places. The basic rule is that anything lighter than your skin tone will make a feature more prominent and anything darker makes it recede. For example, if you want to make a round face more oval or appear to have more pronounced cheekbones, counter with bronzer alongside your face and on your temples, cheek hollows, and chin. It should be a neutral shade without any orange tones. A large or wide nose can look smaller and thinner by using this same shade down both sides of the nose and under the tip. Add a little highlighter to the tip.

- Light and shadow work for your eyes, too. If you have drooping lids, for example, highlighter above your crease, under your brow, will open them up. When it comes to color, stay in the neutral family—browns, grays, and peaches—and you'll never go wrong. Just use a little, though. Again, less is always more. To make the whites of your eyes appear whiter, apply a white or beige liner on the inside rim of your bottom lid. Then add a darker shade such as black or brown along your upper and lower lash line, which will also make your eyes stand out.
- To cover up pimples or any red around the nose, opt for a green-pigmented concealer. If it's too light, it will just accentuate the problem by drawing attention to it.
- Don't over-pluck your brows. They should always be nice and full. A brow mousse keeps them in place but not stiff. Or use a little hair spray on a toothbrush. If you have ash in your brows but gold in your hair, soften them up with a mild product.
- For a naturally fuller mouth, apply foundation over your entire lip. Then take a neutral lip liner and line the entire area. Fill in the rest with color. Lighter colors reflect light, so they will look fuller than using a darker shade that absorbs light. Lips don't normally turn cotton-candy pink, so I like colors found in nature—tulip, melon, peach, or strawberry. Finish with a drop of highlighter or gloss applied to the center of your bottom lip.
- Eyelashes are the one thing you can exaggerate and still look natural. After all, some people *have* thick black lashes. Remember, you don't need a heavy coating on the tips, but getting it close to the base gives eye-opening definition.

Hair Apparent

We've talked a lot about skin, but healthy hair is an important part of the beauty equation. Just like our skin, hair requires care to look its best. Even The Lawyer, with his genetically disgustingly near perfect, frizz-free, salt-and-pepper hair (I hate him!), uses a conditioner every day. However, also like our skin, healthy locks begin from within. The encouraging news is that the healthy, balanced diet that is good for the rest of our body is also good for our hair. Since hair is made mostly of the protein keratin, a diet rich in natural sources of protein is essential. Without it, new hair growth will diminish and poorer hair fibers can result. Also, opt for foods rich in vitamins C and B-complex, and especially biotin (vitamin B_7). Just remember, hair grows slowly. So as you change your diet, be patient—the positive results will come with time. And what makes for a good complexion, such as gentle cleansing and gentle massage, works wonders for your scalp, too.

On average, we lose between 50 and 150 hairs every day. It's not a big deal when you consider that you have about 100,000 hair follicles. It only becomes problematic when you start to lose more than your body can grow. This can be caused by stress, hair extensions, too much heat and chemicals that damage the follicles, or simply a genetic predisposition. When celebrities appear in magazines, movies, and on TV with enviable hair, chances are large clumps of it don't belong to them. Many could probably thank the 4,000 women who make daily visits to a Hindu temple in India, in the hills of Tirupati, to be exact, to take part in a religious ceremony. Called tonsuring, it involves shaving off their hair as a sacrifice to the god Vishnu. One wonders if Vishnu is aware that a generous amount of that sacrifice may end up featured on the *Real Housewives of New Jersey*!

According to Dr. Ryan Welter, a hair restoration surgeon in North Attleboro, Massachusetts, and a pioneer in the field of hair-transplant surgery (who is working to develop techniques using stem cells to improve hair restoration density), several changes happen to hair as we age, including thinning, hair loss, and graying. However, it's possible to experience thinning hair starting as early as your twenties. This type of thinning occurs in a pattern and begins with thinning hair fibers—followed by hair loss—in the affected area. The extent of loss is generally determined by genetics.

"But even people with no history of pattern loss or illness will generally experience some form of age-related thinning over time," he says. "Thick hair becomes thinner and sparser for nearly everyone after a certain age. Eyebrows and eyelashes are also affected. And thick, coarse hair begins to grow in other places, including the face, ears, and lips!" (Just what we need, less hair, but a big fat moustache!)

According to the doctor, graying is caused by a loss of the pigment melanin. As the follicles age, they tend to produce less melanin and progressively gray or whiten. "The onset of graying can be quite variable, though, with some people starting in their twenties. While it can apply to hair anywhere on the body, it normally begins in the temple regions and then spreads over the frontal scalp and back.

Drying and heat can cause damage to the structure of the hair fibers by altering the chemical bonds that naturally exist. By breaking or interfering with these bonds, fraying, loss of bounce and curl, and deteriorating hair health all result. To that end, avoid using chemical dyes or heat too near the scalp where follicles can be permanently damaged.

Hair extensions are almost universally bad for hair and can cause irreversible thinning by a process known as traction alopecia. This form of hair loss occurs from the tension the extensions place on the scalp hair. Hair extensions should therefore either be avoided or only used for brief periods of time.

Here's the promising part! "For most abused hair," Dr. Welter concludes, "the solution can be as easy as stopping the insulting products or treatments. If the follicles are not damaged, new healthy growth will eventually replace the damaged hair." If your hair loss is something that truly bothers you or if you suspect that you have caused damage to your follicles— that is to say that your new hair is not growing in healthy— Dr. Welter suggests a consult with a hair-restoration specialist. There are several medical and surgical options, and more all the time.

Here are my (generally gender-neutral) tonsorial tips:

- Go natural. Save the blow-drying for the special night out. You can control frizz or unruly tresses by using a good daily leave-in conditioner.
- For a deep conditioning, add a little olive or argan oil to your conditioner.
- To avoid stringy ends, regular trims should be a part of your hair-care regimen. For most women, once every three months is optimal, and a week before any major event is recommended.
- Water is just as essential for your hair as the rest of you. Make sure you hydrate regularly by carrying a bottle of water with you wherever you go. Especially on airplane trips, where the cabins are super dry.
- To keep longer hair soft, and tangle free, don't rinse the conditioner out completely. Leave in a bit especially at the ends to lock in moisture and fight fly-aways. Or mist on a detangler with lightweight polymers before combing.
- Remember, here, too, less is more. Don't use a heavy hand with your styling products. A little goes a long way.
- If you live in the northerly climes, consider washing your hair less frequently during the coldest months. Over-shampooing is generally the cause of dull, frazzled hair, and winter weather further exacerbates the issue. For "washing" in between, try using a dry shampoo.
- Excessive blow-drying and flat-ironing will perpetuate dryness and encourage breakage. For overworked hair that needs rebuilding, use a deep moisturizing shampoo and conditioner that contains such ingredients as vitamins E and B_5 to both moisturize and repair the damaging effects of styling with heated tools.

Beauty 9-1-1

Sometimes, despite all our care, we end up with troublesome little beauty emergencies, like waking up on the day of a big event with an acne breakout or having to cancel a first date because a cold sore erupted. While not exactly life-threatening conditions, if beauty disasters happen to befall you at an inopportune time, they might just as well be! So let's take a few of the bigger beauty emergencies and I'll give you the quick fix, courtesy of Dr. Rebecca Baxt, a Manhattan/New Jersey board-certified dermatologist.

- *Cold Sores*—If you pay her an office visit, she will most likely suggest a cortisone injection. Very diluted cortisone injected into the cold sore can bring the inflammation down quite rapidly. If you are afraid of needles, ask your doctor to give you a prescription for topical medication. There are also over-the-counter (OTC) remedies available.

- *An Allergic Episode*—The first thing you need to do is stop applying whatever is causing the reaction. If it's something you've never experienced before, go immediately to your dermatologist. In general, though, for skin allergies use an OTC hydrocortisone cream twice a day; and take a long-lasting (and non-sedating) antihistamine during the day. Or you can try a whole-milk compress for 10 minutes twice a day. To cancel out the redness entirely, use the hydrocortisone cream and then cover it with a green-tinted concealer. A good-quality tinted moisturizer naturally has green/yellow undertones and also provides moisture to dry skin.

- *Cystic Acne Breakouts*—These are obviously much worse than the ordinary, garden-variety pimple. Don't attempt to open the cyst yourself. You not only run the risk of getting an infection but also of scarring, as in a permanent skin indentation or protrusion. Also, if any remnants of the clog remain, the cyst is likely to become re-inflamed and come back even worse. Best to go visit a dermatologist who may inject the cyst with a very diluted quantity of a glucocorticoid, a class of steroid molecules that are naturally produced by our bodies.

- *Puffy Eyes* (from lack of sleep or otherwise)—Apply a cool compress, cucumber slices, or even cooled teabags, since tannins are known to help reduce swelling, for 5 to 10 minutes. These can constrict blood and lymph vessels. Since puffiness can be caused by a high salt diet or alcohol, try to cut out both before an important occasion.
- *Sunburn*—Take a cool bath or shower, but avoid using soap, bath oils, or other detergents that can irritate your skin and possibly make it worse. If you have blisters forming, take a bath instead of a shower, as the water pressure might pop them. When you get out, let yourself air-dry or pat the towel in small, gentle movements. You can also apply cold, wet compresses. Dampen a washcloth or other piece of fabric with cold water and lay it over the affected area for 20 to 30 minutes. Re-wet as needed. Aloe vera can also be extremely soothing, as can cortisone cream. Just make sure your garments are cotton (which allows your skin to breathe) and as loose as possible. Since sunburns degrade the skin's ability to hold in moisture, it can be dehydrating. So it's important to counterbalance this by drinking a lot of water while you recover, at least 64 ounces each day.

All Clear

An important, but often overlooked, part of any beauty regimen has to do with the ingredients in the products we use. In Rung 3—Nutrition, I mentioned that you should read food labels. Well, the same goes for beauty products. Our skin is our largest organ; but being porous, it also absorbs much of what we put on it topically—that also includes our scalps. What goes on—goes in! Thankfully, purer lotions, creams, and cosmetics—like organic food—are proliferating and even some mainstream brands have also hopped on the Green Train, boasting to be free of synthetics and petrochemical compounds. In general, though, a good rule of thumb is to be wary of such additives as parabens, phthalates, propylene glycol, isopropyl alcohol, imidazolidinyl urea, petrolatum, mineral oil, diethanolamine, triethanolamine, formaldehyde, and artificial fragrance and color, especially if you have sensitive or allergic skin. Again, read the labels. Ingredients are always listed in proportional order with highest quantities at the top.

Cracking the Code

Some beauty companies love terms that suggest concrete benefits that don't have to be backed up by science. In fact, as long as they don't claim to change the body's structure or function, companies don't need FDA approval to market new topical cosmetic products to the public, and they are not required to provide any research to prove their claims. So let's start by deciphering a few commonly misunderstood terms.

- *Clinically Tested*—Does indeed indicate that the product was tested, but not what it was tested for! And what were the results? By itself, this marketing claim is meaningless.
- *All Natural*—Doesn't necessarily mean the product is organic or chemical-free. After all, chemicals are "natural," too. And if you've ever gotten a skin rash despite the claim that it's hypoallergenic, that's because they can still contain ingredients and preservatives to which some people are sensitive. The same goes for Fragrance Free. Look for the words "no fragrance added."
- *Non-comedogenic*—Products touting as much are usually oil-free, but many contain dimethicone, which can clog your pores and cause breakouts.
- *Organic*—The U.S. Department of Agriculture certifies organic food ingredients found in cosmetics, but not essential oils or plants used for cosmetic purposes. To carry the USDA Organic seal, a product must contain at least 95 percent organic food ingredients (not 100 percent).

Finally, beauty products and cosmetics may not all have expiration dates, but they can be the breeding grounds for all sorts of nasty bacteria. Here are a few rules to remember: Get rid of any product that has changed in color, smell, or texture. Most skin creams and sunscreens have a shelf life of about a year, but try not to stick dirty little fingers directly into the jars, in any case. Replace loofas, bath, and makeup sponges every few weeks, and purchase a new mascara and liquid eyeliner each season (immediately if you've had an eye infection). Lipsticks and glosses can last for up to three years, but dispose of them right away if you have a cold sore. Eye and lip pencils are good for three to five years. Wash your makeup brushes often. If you have sensitivity to any product, toss it.

Beauty After Chemo

Since my program began with helping cancer survivors reclaim the freedom to always look their best, I will end this rung by writing to them. Interestingly enough, when I give talks to survivors, many women were almost more concerned about how they would look after their treatments than about their own mortality. Aside from asking the initial "Why me?" a frequent angst was "Am I going to look 10 years older?" (My friend Lelia went so far as to ask if she could have a facelift at the same time as her mastectomy!)

I also came to realize there is a large population who suffer from skin conditions induced by their treatment protocol. They have questions about skin care, but these issues are not commonly discussed during doctor visits. So I asked an expert in this field, Dr. Ava Shamban, founder and director of the AVA MD Laser Institute for Dermatology and the Recovery Skin Care Clinic in Los Angeles, for advice.

"Studies have found that patients who feel good about their skin while undergoing cancer treatment are not only more positive and receptive to treatment, but also feel an enhanced quality of life and emotional well-being," she says. "Cancer patients expect to lose their hair, have gastrointestinal issues such as nausea and vomiting and experience fatigue, but they may be unaware and unprepared for how the chemotherapy will affect their skin."

Below are a few ways she suggests patients prepare the skin for treatment after diagnosis.

- *Get a Skin Care Routine*—If you don't have one, now is the time to start. The products you use should be nourishing, fragrance-free, and nonirritating.
- *Block the Sun*—Because cancer treatment makes your skin extremely vulnerable to UVR damage, invest in a good sunscreen or sunblock, at least SPF 25, with broad-spectrum protection. It is important to wear it every day and in every kind of weather, and invest in a wide-brimmed hat and a good pair of sunglasses with UVR protective lenses.
- *Refresh Your Makeup*—Clean out your makeup kit and medicine cabinet. Cancer treatment makes skin hypersensitive and increases the likelihood of contracting infections. Make sure that everything that touches your skin during treatment is clean, gentle, and free of irritants and potential allergens.

And during treatment:

- *Handle with Care*—This is the time to be extremely gentle to your skin. Use cleansers free of drying and irritating detergents and avoid aggressive skin or hair treatments.
- *Go Fragrance-Free*—Anything with fragrance has the potential to irritate the skin during this period. This includes everything from perfume to toilet paper, facial tissue or scented dryer sheets.
- *Use a Humidifier*—A humidifier, especially in your bedroom, is an excellent way to add moisture to the skin and hair. But sure to use one with a good filter and UV anti-microbial features.
- *Wear Gloves*—Hands are one of the most vulnerable parts of the body to experience dryness, cracking, and fissures because they are constantly placed under adverse conditions. Wear clean, dry, long waterproof gloves for all wet household chores and thin white cotton gloves for dry household chores.

Look Good to Be Better Than Before

Even though we've been searching for centuries for the Fountain of Youth through sacred natural springs, snake oil elixirs, and untested tonics, as well as therapies and treatments ranging from the brilliant to the bizarre, there is really no magic way to turn back our biological clocks.

However, we can take better care of ourselves taking tips from all the rungs: Eat healthy by including all the good fats your skin needs, along with boosting your intake of antioxidants; de-stress and unwind; improve your fitness level; get more sleep; and protect your skin from the sun by using a sunscreen every day. Do all that—a little bit each day, week, or month—and I can almost guarantee that you will be more beautiful than before, in every way!

Key Concepts from
Rung 5—Beauty

Concept _____

Why It Interests Me _____

_____

_____

_____

_____

How could I apply it to my life? _____

_____

_____

_____

_____

Concept _____

Why It Interests Me _____

_____

_____

_____

_____

How could I apply it to my life? _____

_____

_____

_____

_____

Concepts to Share

Concept _____

_____

_____

_____

With Whom? _____

_____

_____

_____

Concept _____

_____

_____

_____

With Whom? _____

_____

_____

_____

Concept _____

_____

_____

_____

With Whom? _____

_____

_____

_____

Natural Remedies

"The part can never be well unless the whole is well."
—Plato

Healing the Holistic Way

I started with Rung 1—Doctor's Orders because the advances in medical technology and knowledge are the underpinning of so much of what enables us to achieve optimum health. But as you have undoubtedly noticed through our climb thus far, many of the most interesting and promising developments today are from the world of complementary healing. Therefore, this rung is devoted to holistic healing and other nonmedical ways to prevent and treat what ails us.

Holistic healing can be either allopathic or homeopathic. It is based on the fact that we are extremely complex organisms that have evolved over hundreds of thousands of years without all the medical miracles we now take for granted. This practice works to both fight specific ailments and to enhance our innate defenses, which in turn boost our immune systems. And when we speak of what is called "complementary medicine," we are generally referring to such popular disciplines as massage, chiropractic, herbal remedies, acupuncture, and reflexology.

At the heart of these disciplines is the belief that we all have inherent self-curative powers beyond our medically proven autoimmune, natural fevering, white blood cells, and similar defenses. Indeed, a human being is considered a cohesive whole of mind, body, and soul, closely interconnected with his or her physical and social environment. Therefore, the entire physical state, not just the symptoms, must be taken into account. To that end, holistic practitioners aim to find out everything that is going on with a patient—physiologically, emotionally, and even spiritually. Before making a specific recommendation or writing out a prescription, for instance, they take the time during the visit to better understand the cause(s) of their patients' problems and then explain how they should best take care of themselves going forward.

Holistic practitioners focus on what they consider real health, not just freedom from disease. For example, if you have a headache, they wouldn't necessarily recommend that you take two Tylenol based simply on the symptoms. You would be asked about your stress level, sleep habits, diet, and exercise routines. Although you might still be prescribed a pain reliever, you would also be advised to make certain lifestyle modifications.

Now, I'm not suggesting that everyone will either go that route or wants conventional medicine to disappear. After all, need I repeat that I am bionic from the waist down, thanks to my orthopedic surgeon, or that The Lawyer is still with us due to the stents implanted in his heart? But according to a recent study, the use of complementary-alternative medicine (CAM) by the public is here to stay and growing rapidly. In the United States alone, approximately 30 percent of adults and approximately 12 percent of children are using some form of CAM.

Certainly there are those skeptics who may still refer to complementary therapies as "Voodoo medicine" because of what they consider to be the sheer implausibility of its rationale. But if you had never heard of aspirin and some so-called health expert told you there was a totally natural substance found in the bark of willow trees that when ingested could stop headaches, reduce pain and inflammation anywhere in the body, and dramatically help prevent both heart attacks and strokes—and they had no idea how it works—you'd think they were taking some other kind of drug! So, the next time you feel tempted to pooh-pooh new or unorthodox natural remedies, think of (yes!) aspirin and give them a fair hearing!

Complementary therapies and techniques have been around for ages. Acupuncture in China and Ayurvedic treatments in India both have roots going back 5,000 years. Modern allopathic medicine, on the other hand, dates back to Hippocrates, a mere 2,400 years ago. Throughout that long history, these nontraditional therapies have been known to successfully address such universal complaints as chronic pain, depression, anxiety, and fatigue. Much more recently, they have also been used to ease post-traumatic stress syndrome and stop such detrimental habits as smoking and excessive drinking. And they are currently being applied to help alleviate post-cancer physical and psychological side effects to provide feelings of well-being without negative reactions or complications. The belief is that while orthodox therapies such as chemotherapy and radiation treat the tumor, adjunctive complementary (integrative) therapies such as the aforementioned acupuncture and massage, plus meditation, guided imagery, self-hypnosis, and yoga, deal with the important physical and emotional post-protocol effects. So let's take a look at the most established of these alternatives.

From Acupuncture to Zen Meditation

Get the Point

Acupuncture is based on the theory (or belief) that meridian lines run throughout the body—distinct from the nervous system—conveying Qi, meaning "mind force" or "life force." This energy is thought to exist in all of us as two opposite, but complementary, forces, known as the yin and yang. And it should flow freely along its pathways if good health is to be maintained. When illness or poor nutrition blocks the meridians, these blockages must be located and removed. Therefore, needles made of copper, silver, or gold, depending upon the energy properties of the metal that is required, are inserted at certain points along the affected meridian. Each needle—penetrating only the top layer of the skin—interacts with the meridian to unblock it, which in turn allows the body to repair the malfunctioning organ or body part.

A practice that has been used consistently for 5,000 years must be accorded due respect. What's more, modern science confirms there is an electromagnetic element to the way our nervous system works, based on its atomic and molecular structures. Additionally, numerous studies have shown that acupuncture provides relief for a host of ailments, including pain relief, asthma, and allergies. Acupuncture can be particularly useful if you have multiple allergies, since it works to quiet the areas of the immune system that are overstimulated by exposure to allergy-inducing factors.

Mom's Chicken Soup

My first exposure to the more unusual side of food as medicine was when I hurt my knee when we were living in Paris and the local kinesiotherapist (don't ask) wrapped it in cabbage leaves to reduce the swelling. It worked! But you don't have go nearly that far (or chew on a willow tree) to find remedies in your refrigerator that you might have sought in your medicine cabinet!

In fact, the only natural remedies that presumably predate acupuncture are the myriad of herbal and dietary potions that have been employed for eons. Some are as well-known as, yes, homemade chicken soup, which is very rich in electrolytes, as well as soothing to the stomach due to its mix of warmth and (hopefully not too much) fat that slows down absorption by the stomach walls and neutralizes acids.

Other longtime standbys include peppermint and chamomile teas for tummy troubles, citrus fruits for vitamin C deficiencies, and castor oil as a digestive aid and laxative. (You can also use it around your eyes as an inexpensive, yet highly effective beauty oil. But I digress!) Coffee, tea, and chocolate include varying degrees of members of the theobromine family, all of which are vasodilators (increasing circulation and reducing blood pressure), diuretics, and heart stimulants.

In addition, many other everyday foods have important health benefits. I happen to love kefir and plain yogurt, both created by the work of what are known as "friendly bacteria." Essential elements of our digestive systems, these bacteria are primarily lactobacillus acidophilus and bulgaricus (generally known collectively as acidophilus). The more natural the yogurt, the higher the percentage of beneficial bacteria. Intestinal flus—and the antibiotics we take to combat them and other diseases—can kill off these little friends, upsetting the natural environment of our digestive systems.

The current research involving lactobacilli has led to a major new branch of both medical study and natural remedies—probiotics. Probiotics is the name given to all of the micro-organisms that thrive—literally billions of them—in our gastrointestinal tract. So far, we are just scratching the surface of what scientists theorize these tiny organisms can do for our good health. The focus for this particular rung, though, is on *prebiotics*, the foods that foster that well-being. These include oats, wheat, bananas, onions, leeks, asparagus, soybeans, honey and artichokes, and, of course, kefir, yogurt, and other fermented products that contain the probiotics themselves.

In addition to the above, there's garlic, which is a prebiotic and is also known as nature's antibiotic, and beer, a great source of vitamin B–rich brewer's yeast. These have been forever considered natural remedies. More recently, we have learned that oatmeal reduces the risk of heart problems—although it has a long history as being used to soothe irritated skin. And we now understand why you get so sleepy after Thanksgiving dinner—turkey is high in the amino acid L-tryptophan, a building block for the body's production of serotonin and melatonin, hormones that regulate sleep.

You Had Me at Merlot

Another of The Lawyer's favorite health discoveries is how antioxidants, like those found in the resveratrol in red wine, are heart healthy. I, on the other hand, much prefer the benefits from dark chocolate. Not to burst your bubble here, but both share with beer decidedly *unhealthy* attributes when taken in quantity. That's why more and more companies are manufacturing supplements that provide concentrated and/or purified forms of the essences of these foods and drinks. You can find freeze-dried acidophilus pills and even "acidophilus food" to provide maximal culture-building environments to help rebuild the needed levels. New to this field are products that provide cocoa flavanols—the heart of chocolate's health benefits without the sugar, fat, and possible resulting weight gain!

The following are a few other interesting concentrated herbal offerings:

- *Turmeric (Curcuma longa)*—the root often used in Indian cuisine to give curries their flavor and color. Its active ingredient, curcumin, the subject of 16 studies including 10 human clinical trials, is thought to be both an antioxidant and anti-inflammatory and has shown astounding results in pain reduction, cognitive function, and depression, as well as treating arthritis.
- *Golden Seal*—The root is often used for all digestive problems and as a blood purifier.
- *Comfrey* makes a soothing herbal compress for sprains and bruises.
- *Parsley, corn silk,* and *shave grass* are all natural diuretics.

A cautionary tale: When we first got married, The Lawyer developed a nasty cough. It got dramatically worse over a weekend, and since it was a Sunday, I instead consulted with my guru du-jour, Swami Bobo. Based only on my description of the symptoms, Bobo prescribed the perfect natural expectorant to break up the offending congestion—grape juice laced with cayenne pepper. How was I to know that my husband really had tri-lobar pneumonia? (I thought for a moment that maybe he had three lungs!) Upon being admitted to what became eight days in the hospital, he told the doctor that I had tried to kill him. So natural isn't *always* better.

Get Cracking

Over the years, chiropractic care has become so mainstream that even Medicare covers it to treat certain conditions. This particular form of complementary medicine focuses on detecting, reducing, and preventing mechanical disorders of the musculoskeletal system, especially the spine. It is believed that these maladies affect your general health via your nervous system, something of a combination of orthopedics, physical therapy, and Qi. Chiropractic doctors treat what are known as subluxations, which happen when our vertebrae, due to trauma, stress, or chemical imbalances, lose their normal position and mobility. By applying directed pressure to the spine, either by hand or with a special instrument, the normal position of the spine is restored.

The therapy also works for cranial realignment, a specific technique that aligns the cranial bones. If those are out of whack, major headaches can result. Since it's impossible to directly move or bend bones, unless you are an orthopedic surgeon (or Uri Geller), the idea is that by having your muscles adjusted, the bones will shift into place naturally, without trauma. The goal of chiropractics is to be a noninvasive alternative to surgery. When it works, it is a terrific way to alleviate pain and restrictions on mobility. Of course, as with any other complementary therapy, do your homework to make sure you are putting you and your loved ones' necks and spines in the hands of qualified and experienced practitioners.

Hands On

In many of my columns, I've chronicled how I was able to coax and cajole a frequently recalcitrant male—that would be The Lawyer—into the world of alternative health and beauty. He has stoically undergone having his eyelashes dyed, his eyebrows waxed, and his hair and scalp treated with hot mud from foreign bogs. He has had aches and pains diagnosed through a mind-boggling array of techniques, only losing his preternatural calm once, when a waiter at a pioneering ultra-vegan restaurant on the Left Bank in Paris refused to serve him pepper for his admittedly bland-to-the-point-of-tasteless dish because it was deemed "too exciting."

However, I never had any trouble getting him to "submit" to almost any kind of massage. Massage therapy (or massotherapy) is more than just a rubdown at the gym or a pampering interlude at the spa. In fact, according to the American Massage Therapy Association (AMTA), 38 million Americans a year now have a massage at least once. "A growing body of evidence shows that massage therapy can be effective for a variety of health conditions, and massage is rapidly becoming recognized as an important part of health and wellness," says Dr. Keri Peterson, board certified internal medicine physician, affiliated with New York City's Lenox Hill Hospital and Mount Sinai Medical Center. "Many of my patients come to me with chronic pain, including back and knee pain, as well as migraines and injuries after exercise. I am now referring more people than ever to meet with massage therapists as an alternative, before considering surgery or even prescribing medication."

Recent studies compiled by the AMTA suggest that massage therapy can benefit people of all ages. It can enhance the immune function in preterm infants, decrease blood pressure and improve stability in older people, as well as reduce stress and anxiety in cancer patients. Studies also show that massage therapy can improve quality of life in patients with fibromyalgia and reduce inflammation of skeletal muscles acutely damaged by exercise. In addition, research supported by the National Center for Complementary and Alternative Medicine showed that a weekly 60-minute Swedish massage for those with osteoarthritis of the knee significantly reduced their pain.

But how do you know which massage is right for the condition you have? "To get the best massage for you, consult with your massage therapist to create a custom treatment plan based on your needs and conditions," Dr. Peterson says. "He/she will often use a variety of techniques to help you achieve your health and wellness goals."

Here are some techniques that have achieved widespread acceptance:

- *Swedish*—The most popular type of massage, it includes long strokes and kneading to increase circulation and gently stimulate the lymphatic system and, in any event, should relax you and reduce stress.
- *Deep Tissue or Deep Fascia*—The therapist works deeply into the muscle tissue, actually trying to separate the fibers to both improve blood flow and release the trapped lactic acid that is the natural by-product of anaerobic (i.e., without oxygen—the opposite of aerobic—working the muscle faster or harder than it can work just by burning the fuel in the bloodstream serving it) exercise (what gives you the "burn"). It is also often used for breaking down adhesions and minor scar tissue from muscle damage due to an injury. Deep tissue massage (along with chiropractic therapy) is also considered a helpful complementary treatment for back pain, neck pain, and osteoarthritis.
- *Sports*—Sports massage falls between Swedish and Deep Tissue in depth of work and pressure. It is best used to help prevent athletic injury, keep the body flexible, and assist recovery. It is less invasive than Deep Tissue, working more forcefully to stimulate blood flow and lactic acid drainage in muscles and other soft tissue affected by specific athletic activity.
- *Shiatsu and Acupressure*—Shiatsu is Japanese and acupressure is basically Chinese, but they are both based on the same theories of Qi as acupuncture—with the needles replaced by fingertips applying pressure to unblock the meridians and rebalance the yin and yang forces. (Without the needles! I'm there!)
- *Orthopedic*—A customized approach to orthopedic treatment that can involve various massage modalities, including deep tissue and myofascial techniques, joint

mobilization, and stretching. This type of massage is mostly used to help manage chronic and acute pain. The focus is on improving blood flow and mobility both pre- and post-op and, ideally, *instead* of op.

These are just the best known of the massages; there are legions of others, many of which are at least enjoyable, if not therapeutic!

Good for the Sole

Perhaps the best known form of massotherapy is reflexology, thanks to all the "Reflexology Charts" of hands and feet. It's also known as zone therapy and is one of my all-time favorite holistic treatments. While it claims lineage as far back as 2500 BC in ancient Egypt, as evidenced by hieroglyphics on a royal physician's tomb that show him applying pressure with his hands to the soles of his patient's foot, in this country it became known in the mid-twentieth century. Reflexology is an extension of the Qi philosophy of meridians, based not on repairing blockages where they are found, but from their end-points in our hands and feet. The belief is that dysfunctions in the meridians produce crystal-like formations there that can be detected by a skilled practitioner—and once you've felt the prickly sharpness from what is guaranteed to be merely the round inside of a thumb or other finger, you too will believe it! This alerts the patient and therapist to the source of the dysfunction in the associated body part related to that zone of your foot or hand—ergo the eponymous chart. The massage then encourages that zone to break up the crystal and release the blocked flow of Qi in the meridian.

People around the world claim it successfully addresses a variety of conditions from anxiety, asthma and heart problems, to headaches, diabetes, and menstrual cramps. Regis Philbin passed a kidney stone on the eve of his surgery, he says, due to a reflexology massage. And his reflexology massage, I might add, was administered by none other than my good friend

Laura Norman, author of the best seller *Feet First: A Guide to Foot Reflexology* and the founder of the Laura Norman Holistic Reflexology Centers in New York City, who is basically responsible for popularizing it in the United States. But even if you have no crystals, simply having someone massage your feet for 45 minutes is heaven unto itself!

The Eyes Have It

Much older than reflexology, iridology is purely a diagnostic tool. It is sought by hardcore health enthusiasts to analyze their irises, the colored portion of the eye, to pinpoint sickness or nutritional deficiencies. The theory behind it is that your eyes show how effectively you are eliminating wastes from your system, since any "toxicity" registers in the light-colored rings around the iris.

Each area of the eye, as in reflexology, corresponds to a different part of the body—gallbladder, lungs, liver, stomach, and pancreas. If any of these organs is not functioning properly, certain white, vein-like formations appear in the iris. Also, any previous illnesses, such as rheumatic fever, are believed to show up. Supposedly, it also enables a practitioner to tell how creative a person is. If you picture the eye as a clock, at about a quarter after twelve—in the left eye—there is a slight marking. If that's present, apparently the individual has a creative gift. (I hesitated to ask if I had it!)

Positive Energy

Another twentieth-century phenomenon based on Qi is Reiki (pronounced Ray-Key). Originating in Japan, it is a curative treatment, during which the practitioner tries to infuse the patient with some of his or her own Qi through a "laying on of hands." According to John Kroneck, author of *Reiki Energetics*, we can increase the vitality of our body, mind, and spirit through the energy-based healing of Reiki to combat many illnesses, even one as serious as hepatitis C. He says that the experience of Reiki is gentle, yet profound, and works with your own energy to restore balance and jump-start your immune system. The concept is that if our Qi level is low, we are more likely to continue to be sick or feel stress. Conversely, if it is high, we are more capable of being happy and healthy. So Reiki practitioners allow a high frequency of spiritual energy to flow through their hands to the individual receiving treatment.

Indian Giving

China and Japan are not the only sources for ancient natu-ropathic remedies that are regaining popularity. By some accounts, Ayurveda, which means "life knowledge" in San-skrit, is an ancient holistic Indian medical system that dates to the birth of Hinduism 7,000 years ago in India. In the United States, it is perhaps most associated with renowned physi-cian and author Deepak Chopra, who has taught the tenets of Ayurveda to everyone from Oprah to Lady Gaga. Dr. Chopra says the whole idea is to create balance in the body. "By bal-ance, I mean a return to what in medical terms or biological terms is called homeostasis, self-regulation." He is convinced that "Ayurveda is useful in any chronic illness—coronary artery disease, rheumatoid arthritis or other inflammations, along with bronchial asthma, obesity, and type 2 diabetes, because these are all linked to lifestyle."

Sometimes referred to as "yoga's sister science," Ayurvedic treatments are based on the philosophy that every human being falls into one of three predominant energy body types (dosha)—Vata, Pitta, or Kapha. And its practitioners believe that your chances of developing certain types of diseases are thought to be related to the way doshas are balanced. Each dosha is made up of two of five basic elements—ether, air, fire, water, and earth—and each person is thought to have a combination of the three doshas, although one dosha is usu-ally dominant and a second prominent. An Ayurvedic doctor can determine your dosha just by taking your pulse. An imbalanced dosha will produce symptoms unique to that dosha.

Ayurveda also aims to find the root causes of an illness, such as imbalances related to age, diet, exercise routine, mental exertion, and the seasons. If someone is experiencing doshic imbalances or fluctuations, this will often manifest itself as a physical or mental symptom or disease. Therefore, Ayurvedic practitioners work with their patients to figure out what their imbalances are and then help coach them in making simple adjustments to their diet and daily regimens.

What's Your Dosha?

Here are the primary characteristics of the doshas, according to Anisha Durve, an Ayurvedic practitioner from University Hospitals (UH) Ahuja Medical Center in Cleveland, one of the first major medical centers in the country to offer education in this ancient healing tradition.

- The Vata dosha combines the elements of ether and air and is considered the most powerful. Vata types tend to be thin and lanky and generally enjoy creative endeavors, meeting new people, and traveling to new places. When they are balanced, Vatas are flexible, have lively imaginations, and are original thinkers. However, they can be especially susceptible to skin and neurological conditions, rheumatoid arthritis, heart disease, anxiety, and insomnia.
- The Pitta dosha represents the elements of fire and water, which make them innately strong, intense, and irritable. They tend to have a medium build, and they are competitive, quick learners, and natural leaders. People with a predominantly Pitta constitution are thought to be susceptible to hypertension, heart disease, infectious diseases, and digestive conditions.
- Kapha types combine the elements of water and earth. They have strong frames and are naturally athletic, although they have a tendency to gain weight. They are stable, compassionate, and loyal and prefer a regular routine in their personal and professional lives. Those with a predominant Kapha dosha are thought to be vulnerable to diabetes, cancer, obesity, and respiratory illnesses like asthma.

Ayurvedic treatments include dietary regimens that are vegan and macrobiotic, plus massages and treatments that revolve around the use of essential oils, as in aromatherapy. In addition, Ayurvedic healers use treatments, collectively called Panchakarma, that comprise various forms of, shall we say, detoxification therapies. (Think garlic enemas.) My personal favorite is the Shirodhara, in which a continuous stream of oil flows directly onto the upper part of your forehead. What I initially thought would be annoying turned out to be sheer bliss!

It Makes Scents

Both aromatherapy massage and Ayurveda treatments rely heavily on scented oils. This is another area, however, where modern science has found common cause. "The quickest way to change a mood state or behavior is with smell," says Dr. Alan Hirsch, Neurological Director of the Smell and Taste Treatment and Research Foundation in Chicago, Illinois. That's because, he says, the part of the brain that governs your sense of smell is actually part of the limbic system, or the emotional brain. Happy odors, according to Hirsch, induce nostalgia, for example, baby powder, flowers, or potpourri—especially ones that contain the scent of pine, often a reminder of childhood and a simpler time spent outdoors. "The aroma of roasted or baked goods is always a comforting reminder of home," Dr. Hirsch says. "So make cookies or stick a pie in the oven!" The Lawyer once wondered why I keep a bottle of barbecue sauce in the fridge. Well, it's because if you take a whiff, it is supposed to instantly ward off an anxiety attack. (He was highly disappointed it didn't involve a rack of ribs!)

Massage aside, the bouquets of the essential oils themselves will stimulate the limbic system. Here are a few recipes to try:

- To relieve stress, drip two to five drops of chamomile onto a handkerchief, hold it under your nose, and breathe deeply.

- Using an aromatherapy lamp, a ceramic vessel equipped with a small basin that holds a mixture of water and essential oil that is warmed from underneath by a candle, diffuse relaxing oils such as chamomile, rose, or sandalwood in the morning to enhance your mood for the entire day and beyond.
- Combine 18 drops of lavender with one ounce of water in a mister. Spray four times on your pillow before bedtime for a restful night's sleep.

Quenching the Fire

From time to time, many of us experience acid indigestion and its latest incarnation, gastric reflux. This is also an area where natural remedies can be counted on to help. I wish, in fact, my aunt Ruby had known about it when I was growing up. You see, Aunt Ruby used to frequently get heartburn after she ate little red peppers, and she loved little red peppers—which meant that every time I visited her, I had to witness her grab her chest and announce that she was most certainly having a heart attack. (Hmm, I wonder if hypochondria is genetic?) She wasn't supposed to eat greasy food, high-fat dairy products, or anything spicy, either. (Not that it stopped her from constantly consuming all of the above.) Sadly, when she was actually having a heart attack, everyone just assumed it was indigestion from the fried clams. Happily, she survived to eat again!

Now we all know lots of people who have indigestion and buy OTC drugs to help relieve its various symptoms. These can include not only heartburn, but acid reflux, upper abdominal pain, general gaseousness, difficulty swallowing, feelings of pressure, heaviness or bloating after eating, and stomach or abdominal cramps.

"The problem is, OTC drugs can actually make indigestion worse," contends our friend Dr. Michael T. Murray, N.D., whose many books include *The Encyclopedia of Natural Medicine.* "Take the popular acid-blocking drugs, for example.

They work by blocking one of the most important digestive processes—the secretion of hydrochloric acid by the stomach. While it may reduce discomfort, it also substantially stops the normal body process of digestion. Furthermore, acid blockers are associated with numerous digestive disturbances such as nausea, constipation, and diarrhea."

Dr. Murray says that for people with acid issues, it's smarter to focus on aiding digestion rather than blocking the digestive process with antacids. "Indigestion can be attributed to a great many causes, including not only increased secretion, but also decreased secretion of acid and other digestive factors and enzymes."

The following are four approaches that Dr. Murray recommends to help address the problem—along with his comments:

- *Change Your Diet and Eating Habits*—"Eliminate dietary reasons for digestive problems: overeating, obesity, coffee, chocolate, fried foods, carbonated beverages (soft drinks), and alcohol. Decrease the size of portions at mealtimes; chew food thoroughly; eat in a leisurely manner in a calm, relaxed atmosphere; and don't eat within two hours of bedtime. Chew gum to help promote saliva production."
- *Try Hydrochloric Acid Supplementation*—"Although much is said about hyperacidity conditions, a more common cause of indigestion is a lack of gastric acid secretion. Hydrochloric acid (HCl) supplementation can produce complete relief of indigestion in many individuals."
- *Take Digestive Enzymes*—"Lack of digestive enzymes from the pancreas is another functional cause of indigestion. Typically, when heartburn, abdominal bloating, discomfort, and gas occur within the first 15 to 30 minutes after eating, it is usually due to a lack of HCl secretion. But if they occur after 45 minutes, it could signify a lack of pancreatic enzymes." For that he suggests that we keep in mind that the secretion of pancreatic enzymes is triggered by the HCl secreted in the stomach. "Some-

times taking HCl supplements can lead to their improved release." However, direct enzyme supplements are also available and "the best results are found from multi-enzyme preparations that focus on vegetarian and fungal sources. Just follow the label instructions for proper dosage."

- *Use Grandmother's Remedy—Peppermint—*"Another valuable natural product for indigestion is peppermint oil placed in special capsules that are coated to prevent their breakdown in the stomach. Peppermint has also been shown to be quite helpful in improving gastrointestinal function in individuals suffering from irritable bowel syndrome (IBS), a common disorder of the large intestine. The usual dosage of enteric-coated capsules containing peppermint and caraway seed oil is one to two capsules (200 mg/capsule) up to three times daily between meals."

Mind Over Matter

Nearly all forms of natural healing either employ or amplify tools our bodies have evolved to combat ailments and make us stronger. The two most elemental forms of that concept, meditation and visualization, involve using our minds alone—the one constant throughout human existence, from before there was medicine of any kind.

No Place Like Om

Meditation is an ancient mental discipline from the same Hindu roots as Ayurveda. It is based on the belief that by focusing our entire consciousness on the abstract—whether it is the attainment of Hindu Nirvana or its newer Western Enlightenment version, inner peace—we can channel our will to achieve that goal. For our purposes as a natural remedy, science now supports the idea that people who practice such disciplines as meditation have improved focus, memory, and cognitive flexibility because meditation triggers high-frequency brain-waves associated with attention and perception. It not only provides stress relief, but it has been associated with staving off dementia and Alzheimer's disease.

But it's not as easy as it seems! I once went to a weekend retreat, a rather ascetic Ashram, to learn how to meditate productively. Like many people, I couldn't get my thoughts to slow down enough to reach that peaceful place. Every time I tried to sit still and let my mind rest, I immediately started thinking of things like, did I leave something on the stove, or in bygone times, did I forget to pick up a child at an after school program? If you have trouble, too, here are a few tricks for successful meditation:

- Choose a quiet, calm place with no distractions and assume a comfortable position.
- Close your eyes and begin to relax all your muscles, starting with your feet and progressing upward to your head, concentrating on each part of the body as you proceed.
- Breathe through your nose and gradually become aware of your breathing.
- Select a simple mantra, or just the word *Relax* to say to yourself with each breath.
- If you can, try this form of meditation each day for 10 minutes, building up to 20 minutes.

Dr. Vijaya Nair, author of *Prevent Cancer, Strokes, Heart Attacks and Other Deadly Killers*, has for decades seen the amazing results of regular meditation practice, particularly in lowering symptoms of depression and anxiety, as well as significantly reducing blood pressure in individuals diagnosed with hypertension. Per Dr. Nair, here's a quick technique to do a few times a day for calming a stressed and anxious mind and promoting a healthy heart:

- Place your dominant hand over your solar plexus—on the upper part of your abdomen, between your navel and ribs—and your other hand on the back of your head.

- As you breathe in, let your breath push out the hand at your solar plexus.
- As you breathe out, push your hand deeply in against your solar plexus to expel as much air as possible.
- Repeat for three to five minutes until your breathing is more rhythmical.

Imagine That

After you've learned to relax through meditation, you are ready for the more active technique known as "Visualization" therapy, or "guided imagery." Visualization therapy can be a powerful tool. In its purest sense, it can spur the body's own self-defense mechanisms to act. For example, in a semi-meditative state, you can visualize your white blood cells rushing to fight an infection, or you might visualize a cold virus being chased from your nose, rough patches of skin smoothing out, sore areas feeling good again, or blood coursing to places you think need oxygen and nutrients. This technique also works well for headaches—imagine the painful area being shrunk smaller and smaller, as if the pain had vanished like a wispy puff of smoke. Above all, remember that visualization therapy normally is not a substitute for other curative disciplines, but an aid to making them work better!

Keep in mind, the cornerstone of this Better Than Before program is itself a metaphysical ladder, which is basically a visualization technique. The idea is to grab onto each rung and visualize yourself climbing out of whatever rut you are in and reaching a life that you've always wanted but never thought possible.

Cancer Care and Complementary Medicine

Since cancer survivors were the original focus of my program, I am very pleased that now many doctors and leading cancer hospitals, notably New York City's renowned Memorial Sloan-Kettering Cancer Center (MSKCC), are successfully incorporating forms of complementary medicine and mind/body interventional programs with the standard allopathic cancer protocols as part of their post-treatment offerings.

Dr. Barrie Cassileth, Ph.D., Laurance S. Rockefeller Chair and Chief of the Integrative Medicine Department at MSKCC and author of *Survivorship: Living Well During and After Cancer*, cautions that bogus "alternative" treatments must be separated from doctor-sanctioned "complementary" therapies. Those are the ones that are evidence-based and used to control symptoms and enhance well-being. Nevertheless, Dr. Cassileth still warns that they should never be used instead of conventional treatment. That being said, here are four tried-and-true modalities that she mentions in her book:

- *The Right Foods*—"What you eat matters. It's a simple, perhaps obvious, fact, but one that is too frequently overlooked." The doctor suggests that survivors continue to focus on maintaining a healthy weight by choosing a diet comprised of fruits and vegetables, lean protein, whole grains, and low-fat foods, including dairy. "Replacing carbohydrates and animal fat with vegetables is a smart move, as it has been shown to improve survival in patients with cancer."
- *Increased Activity*—"A flood of recent studies shows that cancer patients who are more physically active tend to live longer after their diagnosis and are at decreased risk of the cancer coming back." She suggests combining yoga with aerobic exercise and resistance training in order to achieve the greatest benefits for both mind and body.
- *Try Acupuncture*—"Research demonstrates that acupuncture can safely and significantly reduce physical and emotional symptoms associated with cancer and its treatment." And while it does not treat the cancer itself, it does help to reduce pain, anxiety, and depression, as well as chemotherapy-related and postoperative nausea and vomiting, hot flashes, xerostomia (extreme dry mouth), chronic fatigue, lymphedema, and peripheral neuropa-

thy (nerve-related tingling or lack of feeling in hands or feet).

- *Mind-Body Medicine*—"The tools of mind-body medicine, such as meditation, guided imagery, and biofeedback, can reduce stress, depression, anxiety, and other negative thoughts and feelings. In so doing, they can help to prevent serious illnesses from worsening, or at least help you through the disease with as little mental and physical wear and tear as possible. Through practice and discipline, mind-body approaches also increase your ability to manage stress."

Dr. Cassileth's advice reflects allopathic medicine's growing acceptance of complementary treatments. But there is also increasing consideration of true alternative therapies. Dr. Karen Turner, for example, a Harvard- and Berkeley-educated researcher and counselor in integrative oncology, is one such pioneer. Dr. Turner had been shocked to learn that despite the medical evidence of the existence of statistically unexpected, or spontaneous, remission, no mainstream institution was studying the cases of people who recovered from cancer without the help of conventional medicine or after conventional medicine had failed. Her dissertation research included a yearlong trip to 10 countries to interview 50 alternative healers and 20 radical remission cancer survivors about their healing techniques. Dr. Turner initially identified more than 75 different factors that may play a role in radical remission. After tabulating the frequency of each factor, she determined that there are nine key aspects involved in documented cases of radical remission: dramatically changing your diet, taking control of your health, following your intuition, using herbs and supplements, releasing suppressed emotions, increasing positive emotions, embracing social support, deepening your spiritual connection, and having strong reasons for living.

Admittedly, it is a long way from such early studies to embracing the alternative treatments as safe for cancer patients to use instead of traditional therapies.

How to Choose a Complementary Health Practitioner

While some of the higher reaches of medicine are becoming more familiar and interested in complementary practices, the general public is still not acutely aware of holistic healers. Many times the words "natural doctor" conjures up images of witch doctors in face paint with pouches of magic powders. However, most holistic experts come in (my dreaded) white lab coats, instead!

While many unconventional methods are not fully supported by the medical establishment as a whole, they are nonetheless making a legitimate impact on the nation's hospitals, universities, and medical schools. Some are truly expanding the frontiers of medicine. But while complementary medicine offers you the opportunity to work with a variety of specialists, including Naturopathic Doctors (NDs) who are licensed in many states and are trained in the basic medical sciences such as anatomy, pathology, and biochemistry, how do you know into whose hands you can safely put your health?

First of all, there are a number of excellent trade and accrediting groups, such as the American Massage Therapy Association mentioned earlier. Others that list practitioners include the American Chiropractic Association and the American Nutrition Association. You also have the right to know where NDs, chiropractors, and nutritionists, as well as MDs and ODs, received their degrees.

In addition to choosing a reputable practitioner, many people wonder whether I recommend seeing an integrated or complementary medicine specialist in addition to their regular doctor. And my answer is always an emphatic "Yes!"

Home Is Where the Health Is

As we've seen, an important part of holistic health and natural remedies is prevention, and that doesn't stop in or on your body. A healthful environment is essential, as well. Robin Wilson, an ambassador to the Asthma and Allergy Foundation of America and creator of Robin Wilson Home, encourages her clients to purchase ecofriendly and sustainable products and renovate with clean construction methods. "Ecofriendly products have come a long way," she says. "They are quite beautiful and extremely durable. And when you factor in the lower levels of toxins, it's the only way to go when furnishing your home." She says that such ecofriendly items as mattresses made from soy and hypoallergenic pillows are all options that don't trigger asthma, allergies, or other sensitivities.

The following are some of her easy starter tips for a healthier home:

- *Begin in the Bathroom*—"Replace your vinyl shower curtain with nylon, since vinyl holds mold more easily and gives off gases. Nylon, on the other hand, is less expensive and repels mold longer and can also be washed. Plus, always use nontoxic cleaners and lower the toilet seat when flushing."

- *Bedroom Ayes*—"For bedding, use hypoallergenic, synthetic pillows instead of feathered ones. Wash your pillowcases once a week, your pillow protectors at least once a month, and the actual pillow once or twice a year."

- *Go to the Mattress*—Your mattress should be nontoxic, and you should cover it with a mattress pad that can be washed. "We spend a third of our lives sleeping, so it is important to keep a barrier between your face and mattress, which typically contains fire retardants and boric acid."

- *Floor It*—Wall-to-wall carpet is a big no-no, as dust mite accumulation can be a trigger for asthma and allergies. "Since walls and flooring are the largest surfaces in a space, make sure to wipe down, clean, and vacuum on a regular basis to eliminate dirt and dust. Also, a good annual practice is to remove everything from the room as though you were moving and clean the entire space from top to bottom. Keep pets out of your children's room and certainly off the bed."

- *Bigger Isn't Better*—Big-city living often means high-rise apartments with thin walls and stale building air seeping in through vents and doorways. If you have allergies on top of this, Wilson says to take extra precautions. "Make sure all windows are properly caulked and that all window unit air conditioners are sealed properly to keep outdoor pollutants from getting in. Use door blockers, draft stoppers, or even a towel at the crack of a door to help maintain indoor air quality."

Other helpful tips from the anti-allergy experts: Use an air filter to reduce pollen or allergens, as long as it's not an ozone generator, which can actually aggravate allergies. And be sure to clean or replace your air-conditioning filters seasonally. The warmer months mean high humidity levels, and moisture is one of the main causes of mold growth. According to the Mayo Clinic, a humidity level of 60 percent or more in your home results in increased exposure to organisms that can trigger a cascade of allergy flare-ups. Experts recommend maintaining indoor relative humidity between 30 percent and 50 percent, which you can monitor with a hygrometer, an inexpensive device found in most hardware stores.

Finally, it is important to make sure your at-home atmosphere is quiet and Zen-like. The Lawyer says my complaining is as bad for his health as my nagging. Kids hate it, too. So never vent when they are around. Otherwise, once they leave, they'll never come back to visit. (Unless, of course, they want to borrow your Amex card!)

Create a Personal Oasis

Speaking of quiet, Zen-like atmospheres, it's helpful to create a space in your house or apartment that you can call your own. Consider it your Better Than Before comfort corner. Keep your private sanctuary truly special by enhancing the senses of sight, touch, hearing, smell, and taste. Research proves that color can strongly influence your feeling of well-being—warm colors soothe, cool colors stimulate. Fill the space with flowers or lush plants in healing green, the color that represents health and harmony. Add aromatherapy candles. For relaxation, choose scents that include lavender, bergamot, or rose. Refresh and revive with the aromas of eucalyptus, peppermint, or cinnamon.

In this at-home refuge you can exercise and work on energizing your inner beauty, charisma, intellect, kindness, and attitude—in other words, whatever makes you, well, you! More important, you can reduce stress and increase harmony by setting aside a short time each day to meditate, breathe, reflect, and use visualization therapy—small moments that have immediate and long-lasting benefits. It is also the perfect place to take the next step up our metaphysical Ladder to Rung 7—Spirituality.

Key Concepts from
Rung 6—Natural Remedies

Concept _____

Why It Interests Me _____

_____

_____

_____

_____

How could I apply it to my life? _____

_____

_____

_____

_____

Concept _____

Why It Interests Me _____

_____

_____

_____

_____

How could I apply it to my life? _____

_____

_____

_____

_____

Concepts to Share

Concept _____
_____
_____
_____

With Whom? _____
_____
_____
_____

Concept _____
_____
_____
_____

With Whom? _____
_____
_____
_____

Concept _____
_____
_____
_____

With Whom? _____
_____
_____
_____

Spirituality

"True spirituality is a mental attitude you can practice at any time."

—The 14th Dalai Lama

Make Your Spirit Bright

Our Ladder has now made us happier and healthier, as well as more nutritionally aware, fit, and beautiful. But are we *better*? That is one of mankind's age-old questions—and a critical aspect of our program. Indeed, finding spirituality and a sense of inner peace is an important part of our journey.

What is spirituality? For most people, it undoubtedly starts with their religious principles, dogmas, and beliefs. In Rung 6—Natural Remedies, we gave Ayurveda and acupuncture credit for having withstood the test of time. Now think of how much respect we must afford our great religions for the support and inspiration they have provided down through the millennia! All one has to do to witness the sanctity felt by the devout is to view Michelangelo's celestial ceiling in the Vatican's Sistine Chapel or enter the soaring vaulted chambers of the Notre Dame Cathedral in Paris or the Hagia Sophia in Istanbul. Here in New York City we have St. Patrick's Cathedral, Temple Emanu-El, and St. John the Divine, magnificent Catholic, Jewish, and Episcopalian sanctuaries, respectively.

It was most gloriously brought home to me when The Lawyer and I were in Bavaria and visited the relatively unknown Ottobeuren Abbey on a dark, drizzly day. While we were there, a wedding was under way in the midst of the abbey's Baroque splendor, its walls and high cathedral ceiling a dazzling concoction of sunlight, blue skies, white clouds and angelic images. Admittedly, I am a crier by nature—I even wept when Nemo was found. So here I was, sitting in the back row, bawling uncontrollably. "I didn't know you knew this couple," my husband huffed, obviously embarrassed that I was making such a scene. "It's just so ... so *spiritual*," I managed to blubber between sobs. Though I was crying, the scene filled me with a bright inner glow, which is, of course, one of the hallmarks of spirituality.

Let's Get Metaphysical

Finding Spirituality in Yourself

Assuming you aren't devoted to your neighborhood satanic cult, if you take your religious beliefs seriously—and by that I mean not just giving them lip service or observing the rituals by rote—you are already a spiritual person. However, for the purpose of this rung, we must also find within ourselves a balance between the world outside and the peace we seek from our souls. It is both an older and a newer concept than those of our great religions.

From ancient times, we have believed in higher powers. This human need to feel that we are all part of something "bigger" and connect with a greater force is the spiritual "enlightenment" to which I am referring. This higher power can be the Judeo-Christian God, the Allah of Islam, Vishnu, Buddha, or your ancestors or loved ones who have passed on. In other words, any deity, spirit, or powerful force beyond yourself, even Mother Nature, combined with a focus on our inner selves. To be clear, you don't have to be Mother Teresa to qualify as spiritual. As with the rest of the rungs, the key is the incremental approach of Kaizen—just to continue to work to be a little more spiritual than before.

A broad, perhaps inclusive, definition of spirituality is that which gives meaning to one's life and enables one to transcend oneself. Whether you choose an organized religion or a more individual practice, each spiritual climb is a personal one.

Finding Spirituality in Good Times and Bad

Our journey starts with making us more aware of our emotions, beliefs, and feelings—as well as those of others. In turn, this compassion, kindness, and concern for all then fold back to fortify us. Thus we should also view this awakening as a part of our psychological growth, in line with the goals in Rung 2—Emotional Well-Being. I also find it a way to satisfy my appetite for wonder. Yes, I do believe in the magic of the universe. To have given birth to three children—and trust me, I am not adverse to having them consider all those hours of painful labor when deciding on a Mother's Day gift—is to understand the miracle behind all creation. And if we look at the world around us with profound wonder, we can begin to slowly conquer the numbness that keeps us feeling low and start to come back to life.

When these children were growing up, each night at bedtime I told them that I was surrounding them with a "white light" so they could go to sleep enveloped in positive, spiritual protection. "Nothing bad will ever happen to you when you are surrounded by this white light," I would tell them. Now, I didn't expect them to believe that they were being suffused in some other-worldly, eerie glow. I just wanted them to feel my love and absolute devotion to keeping them safe and sound. I also fostered in them at an early (pre–Sunday School) age the possibility that there was more to the world than what we can physically touch and feel. And I do believe that without this understanding—and again, in the form in which you entrust your faith—life doesn't have as much meaning.

This belief constantly ennobles our purpose. But it becomes more important during those moments when life seems unfair and we're feeling lonely, lost, or "less than." That's when our spirit needs the kind of boost that that other kind of spirit (in perhaps the form of Pinot Grigio) can't give us! That's where the Golden Rule or karma or yin and yang come in. But we can't always be the one asking and not giving. To benefit from a feeling of belonging, of oneness with the universe and mankind, we have to be part of the good that is out there. And true goodness must come from inside of us, completing the circle.

Of course, achieving that level of inside-out balance, along with the flow of positive energy that accompanies it, can be both impossible and very easy! Impossible if you don't have the will and understanding to do so, but easy once you know what to do. It reminds me of the line in *The Wizard of Oz* when the good witch, Glinda, says to Dorothy: "You've always had the power to go back to Kansas." She just didn't realize that all she had to do was click her ruby slippers together three times.

Alas, achieving spiritual balance and energy may not be as simple as clicking our heels together, but I am convinced that we all have the power within us. We just have to learn how to tap into it. It is certainly worth the effort. Not only will it make you a better person, but it will also be better for your health!

Certainly, the survivors of and sufferers from traumas, even in this age of medical breakthroughs, often find their distress alleviated by their beliefs. Many survivors of grave illnesses have told me that finding a sense of spirituality helped them understand that they were saved for a reason.

In fact, the concept of calling on your higher power to help you through difficult times is not only a universal religious belief, but it is also the backbone of the world's most successful 12-step programs. For example, Step 2 of Alcoholics Anonymous cites: *We came to believe that a Power greater than ourselves could restore us to sanity.* In other words, it "begins with an admission that there is a greater power that can guide our lives, rather than basic desires and feelings. This power has the capacity to help, support, and enable us to overcome our personal shortcomings and restore us to the clean, pure, and happy individuals that we were meant to be." And it doesn't stop there.

Spirituality Makes Us Better

Given the way of the world today, it is understandable that many of us are seeking divine inspiration. Studies show that a positive spiritual orientation not only helps us cope, but also makes us resilient in the face of life's challenges. Political unrest notwithstanding, our environment is also in an uproar, the economy is spiraling out of control, and we sometimes suffer ill health. The world is affected with selfishness, greed, and disregard for life. Perhaps it's this very turmoil that has made each of us want to seek solace in something outside of this world.

Our orthodox religions address health through mandatory practices that may have seemed mystical 2,000 years ago, but we now recognize as health giving. They also provide the spiritual support that modern therapists have struggled for a century to replicate through psychiatry. And holistic healers preach these exercises as being essential to inside-out relief from both physical and emotional disabilities.

The Great Separation

Many still claim that the Enlightenment (with a capital E) of the Renaissance created a separation from our spiritual (and religious) selves that has only grown wider and more destructive to our overall well-being. My friend and expert adviser Dr. John McGrail calls this the "Great Separation."

He maintains that spiritual energy is the energy of Source, your essence, your soul, the energy of the lower subconscious or superconscious. It is the energy of unconditional love, universal consciousness, inner vision, perfection, and divine wisdom. Spirit is the energy of inspiration, bliss, and creation itself; it is the very stuff of the quantum web. Most of us in Western society have lost contact with spiritual energy at some level, which creates the basic energetic imbalance—the Great Separation—that plagues us.

In any of its many forms, spirituality can lead us to where we want to climb. The spirituality of a Buddhist monk or Franciscan friar may be ascetic, while that of a Pentecostal minister or Sufi master may be ecstatic. Hindus may seek understanding of the spiritual plane through meditation, while some Native American shamans use hallucinogenic stimulants. However they—or you—define and search for a higher spirit outside their reality and inside themselves is not for me to say. What matters is that you try to be more spiritual as you advance up the Ladder. Remember, it is the inner self we are working on here, the part that shines through and gives meaning to the accomplishments of the physical and psychological you from all the rungs before!

Seeing the Light

We still must start by turning our attention within ourselves, as if we are looking for a pearl within an oyster. It is, in any event, only your own mind that can touch upon it. Prayer and meditation can serve as the channel to get there. It also reminds us that we are basically seeking the support of a power greater than our physical self and that this power has the capacity to give us continual support through any difficult situation.

Finding the Right Channel

As we look back through time, in almost every earlier era, life was more challenging and dangerous, certainly health-wise, than the periods that came afterward. But they were also simpler and less cluttered. I'm not saying it was easier to meditate when the Mongol Horde was rampaging through your village or the Vikings were storming ashore on your beach. But with no Facebook, Twitter, or Instagram—or electricity, for that matter—quiet time was easier to come by. I mean, would even Buddha be able to sit quietly under that beautiful spreading Bodhi tree for seven weeks nowadays?

I'm also not saying that you have to have the commitment (and patience) of a monk to look within yourself and search for the ever-elusive inner peace. But since we all tend to be too busy thinking about everything else, how can we best go about putting our minds at rest enough to find that deeper comfort?

I asked the Reverend Skye a.l. Taylor, natural faith minister and author, to walk us through the first steps: "Start by focusing your attention on the center of your chest," she advises. "Notice your breastbone lifting as you breathe gently and bring your attention right there. Since we are seeking something out of the daily high-input sensory world, we want to shift it enough to reveal our spiritual 'pearl.' We are, in fact, looking for its light."

According to Skye, the most profound adjustment we can make in our lives is to change our perspective. And when we do this inwardly, the result is even more intense. "Whether or not we have any faith in a particular spiritual tradition, have our own personal faith, or have no faith at all, we can nevertheless turn our minds within to watch and consider what is going on."

Skye feels that much of how we manage outer circumstances depends on how well we manage our inner ones. "Outwardly we are bombarded with all kinds of 'foods' for our tummies, our eyes, our minds, our ears," she continues. "There are just so many options, so many accessories we use for our everyday lives it can get overwhelming. It helps to slow down so we can take control of our sensory input. When we do that, then we can begin to seek within for our pearls of light."

Skye says this process is a key that can offer new insight, a way of finding your own inner light. And this light will have validity, since it's emanating from your very own pearl. "We never have to polish this pearl; we just have to learn how to take control of our minds and our senses, to shift a little from our everyday thoughts. You will see that finding your spiritual side is easier than you think and that your inner light is much closer than you ever could imagine."

I am not suggesting that any of this is easy to accomplish. After all, we are complex beings made up of many parts. What is certain, though, is that we are the sum of all these parts. We have parts that enjoy things and parts that don't; parts that conform and parts that rebel. Skye's belief is that our innate spirituality is the energy and force that bring these all together!

Heart and Soul

For the Reverend Skye, the central pathway to spiritual understanding goes from the conceptual mind to the heart: "This path is the clear path from the mind to the heart, where it rightfully lives. The mind in our brain is merely a function of planning and assessing. The mind in our heart is present and brings us home."

To that end, she suggests focusing your mind inward toward your heart, carefully, watching out for judgment and putting it aside for a while. "Turn your mind in, to your heart space and let it rest there, and breathe. There you will eventually find your way into your own secret garden, your internal landscape that everyone has. In this landscape are all the parts of you, waiting for you to come home and listen to them. Listen kindly. Be very patient, and you will find that your outer and inner lives start to integrate. Peace will emanate from your heart. Your mind will be able to slow down and come into stillness. Don't be afraid to follow your heart. It has been waiting for you for a very long time."

Unblock Party

Of the ancient Hindu and Buddhist beliefs, none are more relevant to our search for inner peace and spiritual balance than the importance of chakras. Originating from the Sanskrit word for "wheel," in Hindi it translates to "wheel of spinning energy." Therefore, they are to be considered the seven central energy points that should be whirling freely in our bodies in a clockwise direction. Yoga and similar practices are devoted to unblocking these critical hubs of energy to clear your path to enlightenment and to ease your general well-being. Much like the therapies we talked about in Rung 6—Natural Remedies, they are designed to unblock our Qi to foster recovery from physical problems and promote optimal health. It is also believed that releasing energy locked up in blocked chakras will prevent the difficulty, or trauma, that caused the blockage from penetrating into the physical body and showing up as illness. Consequently, keeping your chakras healthy and spinning well is key to your longevity, happiness, and well-being.

The seven chakras can be located using a Chakra Chart, showing them in a basic line from the Root Chakra at the base of your spine to the Crown Chakra at the very top of your head. In between is the Sacral Chakra in the lower abdomen, the Solar Plexus Chakra in the upper abdomen, the Heart Chakra in the center of the chest, the Throat Chakra at the throat, and the Third Eye Chakra on the forehead, right between your eyes. According to Skye, the basic do-it-yourself technique for opening chakras is actually quite simple: While you are in the shower or standing in front of a sink with the water running (the flow of water triggering a sympathetic flow of energy through the chakras), you can open each chakra in turn to release blocked energy. You do this by spinning each one in a gentle counterclockwise motion with your fingers. Then run your hand under the water to cleanse it of the negative energy. When you feel the release, then spin the chakra clockwise to set it back in the direction of health. Do this with each chakra in turn, starting with the Root Chakra and ending with the Crown Chakra. Try to quietly feel the full release. If you are successful in connecting with your chakras, after a while you will get a sense of it and know when to move on to the next one. I'm told that in general, a minute at each chakra should be enough. Just be sure to release only one at a time. It is a good idea to keep doing this—it's not a once-only exercise. One time a week is good, more often if you are in a healing mode.

This Is Your Moment

Now that we've cleansed our chakras, we can practice it—or Zen, or transcendental meditation, or traditional prayer—to seek peace and spiritual balance. Undoubtedly, we will turn to it whenever there is any great trauma or difficult decision that interrupts our lives. You may not need this rung to tell you to look outside your daily grind for answers or even for help. What I would like you to do, though, is to recognize that it shouldn't be only in moments of despair when we feel a deep need to reach for something beyond our ordinary mind, to search for a deeper understanding of what this life is all about, and what our place in the great scheme of life could be. We can benefit from becoming more spiritual every single day.

My Golden Rules

I have already noted that I do not claim to have reached my personal goals of spirituality; and if I did, The Lawyer would firmly refute any such assertions! But I do have a number of more achievable goals for you to try along your climb up our Ladder.

Take a Break

The first step toward separating yourself from your daily drudgery is to stop doing it for a while. Of course, if you have become comfortable with meditation, you are there. Those of you who pray every day, especially in your house of worship, are there, too. For the rest of us, though, you can take a break from reality many times every day just by going outside and absorbing the spiritual energy in nature.

If you live in Kalispell or Coronado, that is anywhere outside your door. But even in the stone canyons of our big cities, there should be a park near you; or perhaps a lakeside, riverbank, or coastline. Think about the feeling you get by standing on the rim of the Grand Canyon (unless you happen to suffer from vertigo) or a rocky beach on the Maine coast. You can find a similar appreciation for the wonder of creation anywhere by simply going outside and noticing the amazing variety of living things, the sky above, and the world around you.

Henry David Thoreau, whose classic "Walden: Our Life in the Woods," was a paean to the positive power of Nature, called the support we receive from communing with nature "generative energy."

Turn on a Light

While you are outside or in another comfortable spot, try my favorite spiritual exercise. Breathe deeply and visualize your entire being surrounded and bathed in a bright white light. (Similar to what I gave my children before they went to sleep.) Now imagine this light letting only positive thoughts penetrate while it calms, protects, heals, and regenerates the nerves, the mind, and the heart. It isn't necessarily only about finding inner peace, but it should help you discover the calming space to enable you to move toward it.

Finally, always remember that living spiritually is a daily choice. So surround yourself with visual cues such as short prayers or pictures that remind you of the person you want to be.

Final Thoughts

Our attitude about life steers our journey, delivering us to certain endpoints and outcomes. Our spirituality has to do with our search for meaning and purpose along the way. Spirituality is not something we do, it is something we are. That means it works best when we become aware there is something positive to be found even when times are rough. So, like the anti-stress techniques we've talked about earlier, try to integrate your spiritual life into your daily life. For example, learn to breathe and relax in moments of uncertainty and crisis, seeking the contentment you have worked on reaching.

Know that in this life there are no guarantees of success or failure; it is our own inner peace that guides us through the turbulent waters—and the smooth ones, too. But never despair.

As my wise daughter always says to me when she sees me feeling down: "Don't worry, Momma, everything will be all right in the end—and if it's not all right, it's not the end!"

And that is the perfect introduction to Rung 8—Support.

Key Concepts from
Rung 7—Spirituality

Concept _____

Why It Interests Me _____

_____

_____

_____

_____

How could I apply it to my life? _____ _____

_____

_____

_____

_____

Concept _____

Why It Interests Me _____

_____

_____

_____

_____

How could I apply it to my life? _____

_____

_____

_____

_____

Concepts to Share

Concept _____

_____

_____

_____

With Whom? _____

_____

_____

_____

Concept _____

_____

_____

_____

With Whom? _____

_____

_____

_____

Concept _____

_____

_____

_____

With Whom? _____

_____

_____

_____

RUNG 8

Support

"Thousands of candles can be lit from a single candle, and the life of the candle will not be shortened. Happiness never decreases by being shared."
—Buddha

Spread the Word

In Rung 7—Spirituality, we talked about how essential it is to find inner peace. However, it is also important to remember that we are social beings who need to be with our families and friends. These are the core groups that can help us overcome our physical, mental, spiritual, and social fatigue. To be truly Better Than Before, we must draw support from those around us. As Hilary Clinton put it—"It takes a village."

My friend Barbara told me that she attended a lecture at Stanford University on the mind-body connection, specifically about the relationship between stress and disease. The speaker said that one of the best things a man can do for his health is to be married to a supportive woman (note to The Lawyer). For a woman, on the other hand, it is to nurture her relationships with her girlfriends. At first everyone laughed, but he was serious!

Women connect with one another differently and provide support systems that help them deal with difficult life experiences. Physically this quality "girlfriend time" helps us to create more serotonin, which, as we've already discussed, is a neurotransmitter that helps combat depression and can create a general feeling of well-being. Women share feelings, whereas men often form relationships around activities. Indeed, we give with our souls to our sisters/mothers/daughters, and evidently that is beneficial for our health. It is even said that spending time with a friend is just as important as jogging or working out at a gym. (And I'd much prefer hanging out with Barbara than going on the elliptical machine any day!) In fact, failure to create and maintain quality personal relationships can be as dangerous to our health as making the wrong food choices.

Gender aside, how do we begin to seek support from others? Sometimes we have to ask for help, and sometimes comfort comes from unexpected encounters. This concept was brought home to me the day before my hip surgery. A woman whom I had never met came up to me in physical therapy where I was preparing for the operation. (And knowing me by now, you can imagine what *that* took!) She asked me what time the surgery was taking place, where, and who the surgeon was going to be.

Are you a nurse? Do you work at the hospital? I wondered, secretly hoping that, if so, she would keep an eye on me so I wouldn't bleed out on the operating table.

"No," she replied sweetly. "I'm actually a teacher. All I can do is pray for you. That is what's in my power, and that I will do."

I can honestly say that I was so moved by her offer that I felt it was one of the nicest things anybody has ever said to me in a time of crisis. It truly resonated since it came from a total stranger who wished me well, and would support me in a pure and completely selfless way.

Support doesn't have to be profound or even spiritual to make a difference, though. I also remember getting help from another guiding angel. When we were living in Paris, I was always terrified to cross a heavily trafficked avenue right down the street from where we lived. There were no traffic lights or stop signs, so pedestrians had to wait for a break in the traffic, which was exceedingly rare—and then sprint like hell across the street, hoping that some impatient driver didn't suddenly accelerate and mow you down. Scared for my life, I waited endlessly for the traffic to clear before attempting to cross, which it never seemed to do. One day, a very elderly woman who was waiting patiently on the corner observed my trepidation. "Here," she insisted, holding out a hand and grabbing my arm, "come with me!" Suffice it to say, we crossed the street quite safely, my embarrassment at being led across by a woman who was basically blind notwithstanding.

Strength in Numbers

Yes, random acts of kindness and support can be very uplifting, and I always try to return these favors in kind. But when we are troubled and depressed, or dealing with a serious illness, the most gratifying support most often comes from those who have a shared understanding of what we are going through. Perhaps that's why the supportive therapy afforded by renowned groups such as Alcoholics Anonymous and Gilda's Club (for cancer survivors) has been around for decades. Their members have the same concerns and come together to discuss coping strategies. Having others listen and relate to similar, personal issues give participants a sense of belonging and community, contributing positively to their lives and empowering them to go on when they might feel there is no reason to continue. Many survivors with whom I have spoken have told me that the compassion and understanding they received enabled them to view themselves in a new light.

"It is essential that anyone on his path to wellness surround himself with people who have a great deal of honesty and can show both the positive and negative sides of an illness," one survivor shared with me. "And talking with someone who has gone through a similar health experience can provide hope. Physically, emotionally, and spiritually I may have been through the ringer, but I truly surprised myself that I emerged on the other side a much stronger person." She told me that it was all due to group therapy; and as a result, she now has a far greater appreciation for life and how simple acts of kindness can be healing. "I made new friends who were happy to contribute so positively to my life by understanding that I was suffering as much as they once did themselves."

Remember, though, that it is important to find the right support group for you. When you are in need of a group to help you overcome a traumatic or deep-seated challenge, you are at your most emotionally vulnerable. So, again, do your homework! Seek advice from those you trust. In the case of traumatic illness or injury, this should include your physician. And don't be afraid to leave one group to try another.

If there isn't a ready-made support group available near you, don't give up! You can create your own. As Barbara White, a success coach and motivational speaker in Vancouver, Canada, strongly advises, "Don't try to make changes in your life alone. Gather supportive people around you, such as family and friends. We all need motivation and encouragement when the going gets tough and we feel like giving up. Share your goals with your support network and make the journey together."

Supporting Your Climb

Clearly support and inspiration can come to you in many forms. However, support only works when you are open to accept and benefit from it. That's why it's part of our Ladder—since your Kaizen accomplishments in getting this far should have proved to you that you are on the path to being Better Than Before, and are now ready to welcome in the advice and comfort of others.

A Family Affair

Good health should be a family affair. Your efforts to be strong and fit will influence other family members to do the same. Likewise, your children will best learn to eat right if you set a good example. Dorothy Atalla, author of *Conversations with the Goddess: Encounter at Petra, Place of Power,* suggests encouraging all family members to create a feast for the senses and the heart. "Each person can offer a small gift containing a pledge card with an activity that will unite the family in love and fun throughout the year. For example, a child could propose to collect jokes for family dinners. Another child could volunteer to create skits in which everyone has a small part." Above all, be creative! Make getting healthier a fun game and adventure that all of you can enjoy as you climb our Ladder.

Here are some ideas for ways this rung can work with the ones that preceded it:

Doctor's Orders

Given my commitment to natural health, when I was giving birth to my first son, Alex, I was determined to do it all naturally (albeit in a big hospital). "No drugs for me!" I announced to all who would listen, including, most notably, my OB/GYN, the moment I found out I was pregnant. Of course, that was before I came to realize that this baby seemed to have the world's largest head (think casaba melon) and didn't really want to come out even when his gestation time was up. So, after the twenty-sixth hour of full-on labor (yes, you read it right), I had an epiphany: I needed painkillers!

So not long before I actually started the tortuous hour of actual delivery, I declared to my doctor that I had changed my mind: "I have decided that I don't want to have a natural childbirth anymore. Why don't you just me give me an injection of some sort?" I recall saying calmly; although The Lawyer claims it was more of a semi-coherent desperate plea, as I thrust out my arms, demanding anything to knock me out.

"No," my doctor insisted, "you said you didn't want any medication, and I said I would support you in that. You can get through this! I will help you."

To this day, I was grateful that he let me stick by my desire to have a natural childbirth. And now when The Lawyer—or either of my sons—complains about how much some minor injury hurts, I can tell them they have no idea what true pain is all about. My daughter will learn eventually, though!

Of course, when it comes to following a doctor's orders, receiving support is important in many ways. Take those with type 2 diabetes, for instance. Caroline Bohl, dietitian/diabetes educator at New York-Presbyterian Hospital, believes that whether you have just been diagnosed or have had it for some time, it is essential that you find the right support team. "This will help to ensure that your diabetes, blood pressure, and blood fats are all kept in check, as well as detecting any early signs of complications so they can be caught and treated successfully," she says. To that end, seek out certified diabetes educators (CDEs), health professionals such as nurses and dietitians who have undergone special training to enable them to give patients valuable health information on how to navigate the emotional up and downs, and self-manage diabetes through proper nutrition, appropriate physical activity, medication management, risk-reduction, and glucose monitoring. To locate a CDE in your area, ask your doctor or contact the Association of Diabetes Educators. Check, too, with your local community center about finding local support groups and topical lectures.

Another common medical problem that benefits from a group effort is allergies. This is an affliction for which both allopathic and homeopathic/holistic approaches can work well together to treat or avert—along with medicines like antihistamines, if needed—direct attacks. Getting the support of your family or roommates is essential. After all, even if you constantly shut the windows or vacuum up the dust, if won't do much good if other members of your household insist on re-opening them and walking barefoot from outside right onto your carpets!

That's also why Dr. Atul Shah, author of *Allergies, and Awesome You*, an interactive children's book, feels we must educate, empower, and entertain our children about allergy facts, symptoms, and treatments. "Children with seasonal allergies can, at times, be extremely symptomatic, which can affect their sleep, daytime alertness, and day-to-day functioning. Their quality of life is very much compromised and may keep them from enjoying outdoor activities while everyone around them is having fun." Shah feels the support of family and friends is crucial to helping children understand what allergies are and what they can do to be allergy-free. Information and education are the best starting points.

In short, following a doctor's orders for any illness is much easier when you have the support and help of those around you.

> **Heart-to-Heart**
>
> It is common for patients to feel sad or despondent after heart surgery. Studies show that those who join support groups and participate in cardiac rehab recover faster, both physically and mentally, and are less likely to have future complications. In addition, family members can help loved ones rebound from surgery by encouraging them to take daily walks, resume hobbies and other interests, stay connected socially, and, of course, follow doctors' orders.

Emotional Well-Being

The best support comes from those who benefit from giving it, especially a spouse or significant other. A perfect example of that is brought to us by Jenn Flaa, who wrote *The Happiness Handbook*. The cornerstone of Jenn's philosophy is that most normal, healthy men are hardwired to make women happy. (Nobody you know?) When they get it right, all is well in their world and they feel like a winner, which translates into everything they do. "So if you take the premise that men want to make us happy and need feedback that they got it right," she contends, "that means we women have only three responsibilities in our relationships: decide what makes us happy, communicate that clearly and precisely to the other person(s), and happy dance when they get it right."

Okay, I was with her until that third item! Jenn, who is far from alone in this, firmly believes that men are primarily visually motivated, so a "happy dance" speaks louder than words. For this to work, Jenn says you must show men that what they've done makes you happy—otherwise they'll never know and may never do it again. "Do you let the happiness tingle and energize your whole body?" Jenn asks. "Well, a happy dance is pretty much however you choose to shake your booty."

Frankly, if I did a happy dance, The Lawyer would not only be in a state of shock, he'd go *into* shock! Now, I'm not saying he's not supportive of me already, but there's always room for improvement. And there's no harm in trying, right? So let's look at how this can be applied to the rungs.

Nutrition

With or without a happy dance, there is one obvious way those close to you can be supportive of your nutritional efforts—they don't, to put it bluntly, stuff their faces in front of you. "Tough Love" is not a tactic that makes sense for anyone struggling to change his or her diet. Even the staunchest of willpowers will be tested if you are determined to eat a salad and your husband and kids are chomping on cheese nachos!

Your family must understand that food addiction is a very real problem and is often as hard to treat as smoking, especially with the food industry enticing us into addictive consumption. Why else would modern food processing techniques have placed enormously high concentrations of salt, sugar, and hydrogenated fats and oils into the foods that many of us can't stop eating—can you say potato chips?—if not to keep us reaching for more? So just remember to respect somebody's desire to eat more nutritiously. I'm not saying that your entire family has to exist on your diet of kale or kohlrabi (The Lawyer would say, "Kill me now!") but having everybody on the same rung, as it were, is the best way to continue to ensure success. Of course, if you want or feel the need for further help for getting on or staying on a weight-loss program, there are numerous support groups out there.

Fitness

This is the one rung where support can be both emotional and physical. Being cheered on as you literally sweat through your exercises is terrifically energizing. Just be sure you use the correct words when attempting to encourage. This brings to mind a visit that The Lawyer and I paid to the Rancho la Puerta health resort many years ago. Three days into developing the closest thing he could to a six-pack (his word), he was thrilled to hear the drill team instructor with the heavy German accent finally acknowledge his hard work, barking "Excellent!" as he toiled at completing yet another 20 sit-ups. I felt bad to be the one to tell him that if he had listened more closely, he would have realized that he wasn't being complimented, but rather commanded to "Exhale Up!"

Another appreciated form of support occurs when family members actually assist you in your workouts. There are many great exercise options that are designed for two. Having someone oppose and resist you adds flexibility (again figuratively and literally) to many exercises. But don't stop there. According to Christine King, whom we met in Rung 4—Fitness, exercise should be a family affair. "Work together to come up with a concrete plan, preferably written," she advises, "and then rely on each other to make sure you follow it." You will then set personal goals that you strive toward together, adding both common and competitive elements to your efforts.

Furthermore, there is no better road to fitness success than working out with a buddy. Grab a friend, and be accountable to each other to hit the gym, go for a walk, or attend exercise class on your scheduled days. Your success will improve dramatically!

Beauty

Beauty is an abstract concept—the way we feel about ourselves—but it truly can be tied to the eye of the beholder. We feel more beautiful when others see us as looking beautiful. The balance is in being positive and helpful at the same time. For example, I realize now that my mother meant well and was only trying to help me reach my beauty potential when I was a teenager. Unfortunately, her way of being supportive and instructive instead came across to me as being overly critical.

I didn't want to comb my hair—for spite. So I swore I wouldn't be nitpicking if I was lucky enough to have my own daughter. Those of you who know that daughters take most of what you recommend with exasperated expressions and serious eye rolls realize you must tread carefully.

Good, bad, or a tween, your quest for beauty should be a family affair that also involves your friends. Let them know how much you value their opinion and suggestions, and then listen to them. Just the process of including them in your Beauty Rung—or inviting them into your at-home spa—will add richness to both your climb and your relationships.

Natural Remedies

Natural remedies are still remedies, so you need the guidance of practitioners who are qualified experts. We all know how to intelligently select a medical doctor, whether through the recommendations of friends and family or through traditional certifications. Be aware that there are questionable doctors and alternative specialists out there, so seek the support that is available from referring organizations online and elsewhere, from help groups, and any official licensing board. Remember that faith and trust in your healthcare professional are essential, since successful treatment depends on both your acceptance and your willingness to take the additional steps that are needed to make them fully effective.

Spirituality

I mentioned to you how moved I was by my being told before a major surgery that I was going to be in someone's prayers that day. Well, according to Dr. Keith Nemec, chiropractic physician and founder and clinic director of the Total Health Institute in Wheaton, Illinois, studies have shown that religion, prayer, and spirituality have a positive effect on everything from recovery from acute coronary events needing hospitalization to high blood pressure. One study, he noted, found that people in a coronary care unit that were prayed for experienced quicker healing with less complications than those who were not prayed for. "We see this as one heart, in prayer, reaching out to another heart, physically diseased, to help them heal."

Now that's what I mean by spiritual support!

Paws for Effect

It's not only other humans that provide support—a connection with a pet can be powerful medicine. Some survivors told me that walking their dogs got them out of the house and talking to neighbors. Some adopted a kitten or a puppy that entertained them with their antics and snuggled with them when they were feeling down.

Following the above, I would be remiss if I didn't pay special tribute to my beloved Damian, a 120-pound Rottweiler, a love of my life, who I recently lost at the age of 12. He was, in fact, my child with four legs and fur. Damian was the sweetest dog in the whole world and had the best heart. We were always amazed when others would first meet this enormous black beast with the intimidating rust-colored mask, not to mention inch-long canines, and coo, "What an absolutely adorable dog!" He just gave off a wonderfully sweet aura. And yes, I do believe that dogs have souls.

Damian was, above all, a tremendous source of emotional support for me in his unquestioning devotion and loyalty. Even if it meant we were constantly tripping over his giant dark body, virtually invisible at night because he parked himself in the most strategic spot to guard us all. When our nest became officially empty, having a warm loving being to nuzzle with and dote on was amazingly rewarding emotionally!

Of course, another wonderful quality about pets is that, unlike your mother, they never judge you. I could complain about anything to Damian, and he would never love me any less. (And if it came with a Beggin' Strip, he would love me even more.)

Internal Support

Sharing your stories is extremely therapeutic because what you receive in return proves that you are not alone. Nevertheless, not everyone is willing to share their angst with the world, even though in support groups one's privacy is very much respected. For those uncomfortable to admit their weaknesses and fears, it's also possible to work on ways to support ourselves. Says my friend, public relations executive Sandra Sokoloff, "While I always appreciate external support and know support networks are important to affecting changes in health habits, perspectives, and attitudes, I believe we must create our own internal support systems, an internal trainer if you will, for change to really take root."

For Sandra, this emotional workout took the form of a physical training routine. "I get up and push even when I'm not experiencing success or seeing results. I prohibit indulgent behaviors (binging on ice cream, staying in bed all day), and I don't slack off because I'm in 'training.'" Even when she can't see the goal, she knows it's out there. "I do have 'feeling sorry for myself' time outs on occasion, but it's with the understanding that I have to get back up. I believe my internal trainer is the source of my strength and success."

A Special Note for Cancer Caregivers

As you know, I have spoken a lot about cancer in previous rungs, in no small part due to the fact that the trials and tribulations of survivors were the original reasons I developed the Ladder. There is no one-size-fits-all psychological counseling for survivors, since everybody's personality is different. But the one complaint most survivors seem to have in common is that their cancer ordeal has left them so unsettled that they have to be better prepared psychologically just to get through a normal day. Many suffer feelings of inadequacy—"Am I ever going to be as productive as I once was?" "Am I damaged goods?" "Will the person whom I love—or someday hope to meet—desire me after all this?"

In particular, women seem to have self-esteem issues. By lacking confidence in their skin, hair, and body, they had lost much of their sexuality and sense of self. Common comments were—"I want to start to feel special." "I want my confidence and femininity back." Or, "I feel that my body has betrayed me."

Indeed, the once ordinary situations they used to take for granted have now become stressful for some and overwhelming for others—for example, sleeping, eating, socializing, sex, or just the enthusiasm to go out and enjoy their day. Many are overwhelmed by a dark negative energy that cancer leaves behind that affects many survivors but is seldom discussed in public. As I've mentioned, these cancer demons or CDs can play over and over again in survivors' minds and seem to be there only to remind them that they once had cancer, and it will always be a part of their lives. The antidote has everything to do with support.

The mission of these CDs, you see, is to give you those disturbing thoughts or voluntary or involuntary actions such as touching the area where the cancer first presented. In some cases, you won't even know the demons are there as they can act insidiously by making it difficult to go to sleep, waking you up in the middle of the night for no apparent reason, or just plain give you a feeling of dread that the cancer will come back—or that it never left. They might also cause survivors to overreact or become hyper-alert to any change or the most mundane of everyday occurrences.

Burdened as they are with the unpleasant memories of their treatment protocols and, in many cases, near-death concerns and survivor's guilt, cancer survivors (and those of other similarly life-altering diseases and traumas) have the challenge of finding the inner strength to battle these CDs alone. Therefore, the role of caregivers becomes even more important. In fact, the job is so vital and demanding that there are numerous support groups for the caregivers themselves! Of course, many of the more debilitating issues may require advanced care professionals, such as psychologists and psychiatrists, so don't try to do too much on your own!

As with the stages and levels of recoveries, caregiving has a range of responsibilities, starting with basic physical assistance. But as the survivor climbs his or her rungs to being physically healthier, the job evolves, requiring a greater focus on the emotional and spiritual to re-create, or create, a more satisfying quality of life. And remember our mantra of Kaizen in this, as well. Supporting a cancer or other major trauma survivor can be a slow and frustrating process, as dealing with mental burdens often is. But as you build trust with a survivor, the rewards are amazing.

Caregivers might start by asking about fears and concerns. And as almost all professionals in this field will tell you, never minimize them! Unless you've been in their shoes, it is impossible to know how oppressive their burdens can be. But you can try to help them work through the CDs. Help them understand that thoughts have power—thoughts can create reality. For example, ask them to try this: If those little voices start to bother you first thing in the morning, telling you that your aches and pains are a lot more than aches and pains, don't indulge them. Brush them aside by simply saying, "Look, we've played this silly game before. Come back a little later in the day when you have something new and I have a little more time to dance with you."

And then someday it may turn into a Happy Dance.

Family Ties

A magazine interviewer once asked me who my biggest supporters were. I didn't hesitate to respond—my family. The Lawyer, while not exactly a paragon of healthy living, what with his three coronary stents, his love of rare sirloins, and his low HDLs, is making a huge effort to eat less fat and exercise more. And he is still the most positive and honorable person I know—a supportive husband, father, and grandfather.

In return for all his kindness, how do we support him, you ask? Well, he loves to tell stories. They are often about himself or tales we have all heard before, usually involving the kids (and which the kids are mortified to hear yet again). But we still make a group effort to listen and show how much we love him.

The point being, family should be supportive of our endeavors, even if that means putting aside our own preferences once in a while. At the end of the day, support is without question a two-way street. Rung 9—Giving Back is therefore the perfect plateau to our climb.

Key Concepts from
Rung 8—Support

Concept _____

Why It Interests Me _____

_____

_____

_____

_____

How could I apply it to my life? _____

_____

_____

_____

_____

Concept _____

Why It Interests Me _____

_____

_____

_____

_____

How could I apply it to my life? _____

_____

_____

_____

_____

Concepts to Share

Concept _____
_____
_____
_____

With Whom? _____
_____
_____
_____

Concept _____
_____
_____
_____

With Whom? _____
_____
_____
_____

Concept _____
_____
_____
_____

With Whom? _____
_____
_____
_____

Giving Back

"The smallest act of kindness is worth more than the grandest intention."

—Oscar Wilde

Many Happy Returns

Giving Back is our highest rung because it is made possible by everything you've done so far. It belongs at the top of the Ladder, not because you have incurred a karmic obligation to repay or compensate any specific person or society at large for the benefits you've received. But because doing so is the culmination of your journey to becoming Better Than Before!

We have all heard the old adage "It's better to give than to receive." Well, research shows that giving to others can trigger feel-good endorphin responses similar to those of high-intensity exercise. But for us, and our climb up the Ladder, it reflects a higher meaning—that the physical, emotional, and spiritual energy we have achieved during our Kaizen climb reaches its peak if we share information, challenges, and successes with others.

One of my favorite quotations is from Thornton Wilder's *The Angel That Troubled the Waters*: "In love's service, only wounded soldiers can serve." Now, far be it from me to suggest that we must suffer a serious illness in order to provide help and support to others who have been ill. (Your oncologist doesn't have to have had cancer in order to treat you, right?) So Wilder's line can also be taken to mean that the struggles we experience afford more insights than our successes. The fact that we have come this far up the ladder gives us the power to assist those just starting out.

I firmly believe that where your consciousness goes, your consciousness grows.

For me personally, as that long ago fortune teller had predicted, helping others achieve a renewed sense of self, energy, and enthusiasm for life did, in fact, become my mission. It was a huge undertaking and continues to be a work in progress. But judging by the feedback I have received, it is a gift that has kept on giving. One survivor told me that after following my advice, she learned to accept her physical side effects and view herself not as a cancer "victim" but as a "victor." She also realized that she was now in a position to pass along her strength to those who needed it most, and she wanted to make a difference by helping other survivors. Needless to say, I was extremely humbled by how meaningful our journey had been to her.

Another basic principle of the Better Than Before program is that in order to keep the positive feelings you develop, you must also be willing to give some of them away. As Oscar Wilde also said, "giving back to others can often elicit an unexpected act of kindness in return." For example, the next time you see someone on the street that looks like a big sourpuss, simply smile at him or her. You'll see that more often than not, your warm vibes will be returned.

After all, it's the little things in life that can add up to make a bigger impact, whether it's saving one little tree—or one little psyche. Or one case of mistaken identity! Allow me to explain: A while ago, I took my Damian to the local dog run. It's usually pretty crowded, but that day the only other visitors were an older man in a baseball cap and sunglasses and his large poodle. As the dogs played, the man and I spoke. I told him all about the Ladder. He said it was very timely, since he had to go to the doctor for a checkup the next day. He had some coronary and prostate issues, among other things, and was scared to death of the visit.

During our conversation, I asked him about his diet, exercise program, state of mind, and what tests he would be taking. We even somehow got on the subject of what he should do to make his wife happier. I gave him a ton of advice, and then we both said good-bye and left the park.

Two weeks later, I was walking Damian down a path by the water, and who should come along but the guy from the dog run wearing the same cap and sunglasses. This time, though, he didn't bring his poodle. We said hello to each other, as we happened to be walking side by side. I then launched into a conversation that went something like this …

"So, did you see your doctor?" I asked

"Yes!" He responded.

"And? All good?"

"As a matter of fact, everything is great!!"

"Wonderful news," I enthused. "Your prostate is normal?"

"Yup."

"Heart okay?"

"Never better!"

"Are you eating asparagus for your kidneys?"

"I am. I love asparagus!!"

"Using essential oils to massage your wife's feet?"

"Always! She just loves foot massages."

My inquisition kept up, interspersed with advice from all the rungs, until we reached a fork in the road and he started to turn off.

"Nice to have spoken to you," he said. "Thanks for caring! It made my day!"

"Happy to have helped," I responded, and then added, "By the way, how's your dog?"

He paused, seemed puzzled and finally spoke: "What dog? I don't have a dog!"

Suffice it to say, I had been grilling a total stranger who must have thought I was either a total saint—or a total nut job. I mean, who asks a random person you bump into on a walking path about the oils he uses on his wife—or the condition of his prostate? But after I explained the situation, he had a good laugh at the confusion and said he would start his own "climb" that very day. So whether it was indeed kismet or karma, it made me feel better knowing that I had launched another person on his way to becoming better than before!

Money-Back Guarantee

Some forms of giving back are obvious. Volunteering at the clinic or charity that either helped you or appeals to you is a great way to share. The important thing is giving of yourself, not your bank account. Supporting these causes financially is clearly valuable for the good it does, but by itself, it doesn't make you better! That comes from sharing what's inside you.

So how should we best board the giving train? I put that question to Louix Dor Dempriey, a spiritual master who has spent decades teaching people to become happier through his seminars, workshops, and eponymous retreats. Louix says the first thing you need to do is to "surround yourself and associate with those who share and support your beliefs, dreams, and visions." This will help you feel sourced, inspired, and will create a sense of belonging. With that as your base, here are his six suggestions for giving back:

- *Practice Gratitude*—Start and end each day by expressing gratefulness for everything in your life—including and especially for your "have not's," your pain and suffering, and even for your adversaries, for these are our greatest gifts and greatest teachers. "Gratefulness is the highest form of prayer."
- *Practice Forgiveness*—This is one of the most overlooked, underutilized, and yet most powerful tools that exists for creating happiness in life. Equally as important as forgiving others is the need to forgive oneself.
- *Surrender Control*—The fear-based need to control others, control one's own life, and control one's circumstances always and only brings unhappiness, in addition

to being completely futile in the first place. You cannot push a river.

- *Become More Tolerant and Accepting*—Like snowflakes, no two humans are alike—not even identical twins. Yet we were all created equal, and we all have certain rights and freedoms. As you allow others to express themselves as you would want that same freedom granted to you, you will find happiness growing inside yourself.
- *Become More Honest and Accountable*—When people stop deceiving themselves and others, when they stop living in denial and avoidance, and take ownership of their words, feelings, and choices, a freedom that breeds happiness results.
- *Bless Everyone and Everything All the Time*—Believe it or not, the simple act of blessing everyone and truly being happy for their wins and successes brings untold blessings and happiness into your own life.

Circles of Giving

Another tried-and-true expression is "Charity begins at home." We are told on every airline flight to put the oxygen masks on ourselves before helping our "accompanied minors" (presumably so you won't pass out in the process). Therefore, our giving back will only go beyond the superficial—as in simply writing a check—if it comes from a warm place inside. So, perhaps ironically, taking care of yourself, mentally, physically, and spiritually will allow you to give back to your family and others in more fulfilling ways. For instance, if a sick or injured family member really needs you, how can you expect to help him or her if you're not well yourself? Not only should you be a role model, but as everyone notices the improvements you are making to your own life as you journey up the rungs, it will inspire him or her to join you on your climb.

Think of yourself as a pebble splashing into a pond, setting off ever widening circles. Start giving back to those closest to you, for example your immediate family members. Then work outward to include your caregivers, your friends, and then your community as the ripples move farther away from you!

Family First

Those nearest and dearest to you are the ones you can affect most easily, most often, and most of all. Begin by making it a point to always exude positive energy when you are around them. That means no screaming, complaining, or muttering shameful things under your breath when you are angry. Be sure to invite them to climb with you. The payback will be two-fold: You will receive the benefits of sharing your accomplishments with them, and they, in turn, will share theirs with you.

Believe me, I understand it's not easy to be supportive of someone who doesn't always listen to you—and it's not necessarily your teenage children!

As I've already mentioned, The Lawyer loves to cite the study that found that nagging spouses (who me?) can cause greater stress than most anything else. So when he went to the hospital for his second (and third) stent, I remember the nurse chirping, "Hello, Mr. Michael, what brings you here again?" I grumbled, "His lifestyle!"

I think the lesson here for giving back is to have patience. If somebody doesn't want to adopt healthy habits, you can only *suggest* change, you can't force it. "The stars impel, they don't compel," is one of my most often cited mantras. Still, there are many ways to give back to our family every day, from preparing healthy meals and encouraging good habits, to simply listening and supporting their endeavors. (Of course, the occasional foot massage doesn't hurt either!)

"Having a healthy heart is a family effort," says Dr. Coral Arvon, director of Behavioral Medicine at the Pritikin Longevity Center + Spa in Miami, Florida, which specializes in helping cardiac patients live better. "Every member should work toward that goal. Start by being more positive, and make it a point to walk, take yoga classes, or even practice relaxation exercises together." Family members provide encouragement, but, in the process of giving, also reap benefits.

Caring for Your Caregiver

When you think about it, every one of us has been cared for at some point in our lives, which means we all have an opportunity to give back to someone. Of course, those who take on the role of caregiver during an illness deserve special attention. That being said, many survivors aren't aware of just how much their caregivers have sacrificed for them. And research proves that patients with caregivers have a much higher rate of survival than those who have to manage on their own. However, from the caregiver's perspective, all this dedication can have both a physical and a mental downside. There is even a term for it in the medical community—Caregiver's Syndrome.

For example, a survey shows that 80 percent of cancer caregivers experience regular distress and sometimes don't even realize it. The emotional side effects can include burnout, frustration, anger, emptiness, insecurity, resentfulness, and depression. Physical symptoms can take the form of headaches, insomnia, backaches, fatigue, lingering colds, stomach upsets, or even cardiovascular problems.

To help make caregivers feel better than before, here are a few simple suggestions for how you can give back to them on each of the rungs:

- *Doctor's Orders*—Make sure your caregivers don't neglect their own health by keeping their doctor and dentist appointments, and having yearly check-ups.
- *Emotional Well-Being*—Help your caregivers recognize that your problem may have left them with their own set of issues. Reassure them that they, too, will eventually be able to overcome them as you both get healthier by climbing up the Ladder. And just in case they have any

negative feelings about all they have done for you (and they will, trust me), suggest they write them down in a place where you can't read them.

- *Nutrition*—Set a good example by slowly adding some of the suggestions from Rung 3—Nutrition to your daily menu. You both will benefit from better eating habits.
- *Fitness*—Remember that physical activity helps the emotional life. Suggest that your caregiver does easy exercises with you. You might also encourage them to walk with their friends or join a health club. Remind them that people who exercise regularly are less likely to get sick.
- *Beauty*—For a female caregiver, give a gift certificate for a makeover, including a new hair color, cut, and style and even a makeup lesson. For a male, buy a gift certificate to a favorite clothing store and suggest that he choose something that will flatter his appearance. (If he's like The Lawyer, to ensure that, make sure you go along!)
- *Natural Remedies*—Don't ask. Just book an appointment for your caregiver to have a massage or reflexology session. It's a great jump-start for relieving stress, and it will let them know that you understand how stressed out they are because of what they did for you, and how much you appreciate it.
- *Spirituality*—Open up our heart to show that their care has moved you and that their good acts increase all the goodness in the world, not just your current travails.
- *Support*—Insist that they not feel guilty about asking other people to help take care of you so they can have some personal time.

Pet Projects

I need to make a special mention in this rung, too, for the most loyal and selfless of companions, our pets—at least our dogs (cats are generally more, well, independent!). So it is only right that we take care of our puppies until the very end. For advice on how dog owners can be more proactive in their pet's health,

I turned to Dr. Liz Hanson, practicing veterinarian at Corona Del Mar Animal Hospital. "As far as senior dogs, it's important to begin preventative care before your dog shows visible signs of aging, such as limiting the amount of high-impact exercise and beginning a supplement routine. Pet retailers now offer glucosamine chondroitin supplements and treats that also help build joint cartilage, lubricate joints, and strengthen muscles around the joint tissue, increasing mobility and easing discomfort. There are also products out there for their joints, heart, and brains to stave off doggy dementia."

In addition, feed them an appropriate diet to maintain lean body conditions. Restrict calories for less active dogs because obesity often leads to exacerbated joint pain. The best forms of exercise for older dogs are controlled leashed activity and swimming. This will help prevent most orthopedic injuries and reduce extra strain on arthritic joints. Trim their nails regularly; and to maintain shiny, healthy coats, bath them often and supplement with omega-3 fatty acids.

Community Outreach

Once you've started giving back to those you know, you are ready to expand your circle to the community. There are no rules for this, however. After reaching this rung you will have developed your own sense for what is important to you, and how to share your inner spirituality and accomplishments with those who will best benefit from your outreach. So whether you volunteer at your church, synagogue, or the PTA, or join a survivors' help group (a great one is LIVESTRONG® at the YMCA, which helps adult cancer survivors reclaim their health and well-being following a diagnosis)—or anywhere else—make it your goal to find a way to feel better by doing good!

For example, if you are a cancer survivor, the purpose doesn't have to be cancer related, but since you have special expertise in this area as a "wounded soldier," you might like to assist others who have just been diagnosed. Often your physician or hospital will encourage this interaction and be happy to provide you with the connection. You will see that networking with the newly diagnosed can be an extremely empowering strategy.

The reverse is also true. If you are newly diagnosed with cancer or another serious affliction, letting a survivor mentor you will help you both. Often a person who has survived cancer gains a sense of meaning and purpose in doing something for others with the same disease. This is a remarkably important way of giving back because seeing and talking with someone who has beat the odds and survived your type of cancer is a more tangible sign that you, too, can survive. It is truly a gift of hope and can be given only by someone who has been there.

It's Easy Being Green

The final circle is the world we all live in. Being a native and lifetime Manhattanite, I'm not going to presume to give you profound ecological advice. But as a health, fitness, and beauty expert, I am acutely aware and concerned about the toxicity of our environment—especially for us city dwellers. Yes, modern science and industry have made unbelievable advances in our quality-of-life. But it came with the price of both direct pollution and the more subtle long-term concerns from all the chemicals we encounter every day with which evolution has not prepared our bodies to deal.

So to give back in a way that seeks to extend the internal health and natural balance we've been cultivating in our climb, be kind to Mother Nature. Going green is no longer a trend, it should be a lifestyle. Reuse, recycle, and compost. Learn as much as you can about cleaning up our food and environment, and the knowledge will go a long way in helping all of us live healthier lives.

John Cronin, senior fellow for Environmental Affairs at Pace Academy for Applied Environmental Studies, says, "There are two questions I am asked most often: 'Can one person really make a difference, and how?' The answer to the first is easy: Yes! It is the story of human history—but those who never try to make a difference never do." Cronin poses a creative challenge: "Look to your own life to find that something special that you can make happen." For example, help your child's school find environmental experts to speak to classes. Here's a simple idea: Share a fascinating fact, and your friends will spread the information, too—how much of the water on our planet is available for drinking? (Answer: Less than 1 percent). I promise they will be amazed, educated, and eager to tell someone else.

The point is that in addition to our individual behavior, there are creative acts you can perform, invent, and organize that will change the world right in your own backyard if you are bold enough to try. The planet is also waiting to become better than before.

Better Businesses

I have to also acknowledge that the concept of giving back is not limited to individuals. There is a whole new trend called Corporate Social Responsibility. Today, there are many enterprises, from inside the healthcare world or not, that are giving back to make the world a better place. Giant companies such as Express Scripts are developing wellness programs for their employees, as well as their members and consumers. And publications such as *Town & Country* magazine, where my own quest first began, have been unwavering in chronicling the impact of philanthropies on modern society.

Another stellar example is Canyon Ranch, one of the nation's leading health and wellness facilities. Twenty-five years ago, Canyon Ranch took note of the fact that those at the lowest income levels are usually faced with the highest incidences of obesity, chronic disease, infection, and cancer. Between a lack of health literacy and access to health care, they are then forced to struggle to find adequate resources. So they started the Canyon Ranch Life Enhancement Center—called "the ultimate expression of the Canyon Ranch mission" by founder, Mel Zuckerman. The center is a sheltered environment within Canyon Ranch where guests who need to develop healthier lifestyles can find every possible resource for lasting change.

In 2002, Zuckerman also started the Canyon Ranch Institute (CRI), a goal of which was to adapt the Canyon Ranch Life Enhancement Center's acclaimed preventive health program for residents in the world's most disadvantaged neighborhoods. Program participants report experiencing a number of healthy changes, including socializing more, exercising at home, feeling less pain, increased ability to manage stress, relaxing and meditating, eating healthier foods and healthier portions, and feeling less depressed.

Beauty Products with a Purpose

Robin McGraw, wife of the iconic Dr. Phil, has an impressive fan base of her own—millions of women who turn to her for guidance and direction. With both passion and compassion, she has made it her life's work to comfort and support them, especially those dealing with life-challenging issues.

Robin has dedicated her Robin McGraw Revelation lifestyle brand to her beloved mother, Georgia, who had a tragic and untimely death from a heart attack when she was only in her fifties. It became Robin's revelation: Her mother, while devoting her entire life to her family, had not taken proper care of herself. Robin realized that loving your family and neglecting yourself are not the same thing. If a woman loves her family, she must not—and should not—neglect herself.

Robin honors her mother through her philanthropy, as well. Profits from select products support "When Georgia Smiled," her domestic-violence prevention and education foundation, which creates and advances programs to help women and children live healthy, safe, and joy-filled lives. Her inaugural program, The Aspire Initiative, was conceived to educate a wide-range of audiences on domestic violence issues, from prevention to safe exit strategies. It features a potentially lifesaving smartphone app and domestic violence curriculum, both available free of charge.

Share the Good Feeling

Finally, it is important to learn to feel good about yourself by doing positive things for others. This means helping people realize that happiness is making the most out of every second of the day, and that contentment comes from having an objective and ultimately realizing it. It's about forgetting yesterday, not sweating tomorrow, and making the most of today!

Most important, remember to pass on the love that has been given to you. My own family has taught me what that's really all about. In a nutshell, loving those closest to you supersedes wealth or privilege. It's about giving, not receiving, sharing and forgiving, and loyalty through good times and bad. As for your children, you'll be pleased to know that all the sacrifices you have made on their behalf and all the goodness you have instilled in them will come back to you one day, I promise.

Key Concepts from
Rung 9—Giving Back

Concept _____

Why It Interests Me _____

_____

_____

_____

_____

How could I apply it to my life? _____

_____

_____

_____

_____

Concept _____

Why It Interests Me _____

_____

_____

_____

_____

How could I apply it to my life? _____

_____

_____

_____

_____

Concepts to Share

Concept _____
_____
_____
_____

With Whom? _____
_____
_____
_____

Concept _____
_____
_____
_____

With Whom? _____
_____
_____
_____

Concept _____
_____
_____
_____

With Whom? _____
_____
_____
_____

Better Than Before
Forever More

"Ever drifting down the stream. Lingering in the golden gleam. Life, what is it but a dream?"
—Lewis Carroll

We have come to the end of our climb up the metaphysical ladder. But that doesn't mean that your journey is over. I hope you now realize that you have the wisdom, the power, and the courage to see the light through any darkness and follow your dreams—and your passions—to change your life for the better. Try to include suggestions or inspirational advice from each of the nine lifestyle disciplines every day. When followed systematically and in combination, each rung will become a commanding force that will give you guidance and encouragement, which lead to hope and a renewed sense of self, energy, and enthusiasm.

Know that consistent, steady movements and improvements are what count. The smallest step you can take to move forward that day—that minute—is all that is needed to take the big step toward looking and feeling Better Than Before. And once you see how good you will feel, making just a few little tweaks at a time, you will never want to go back to your old habits or way of life.

I hope, too, that you have come to understand that life is not only about living longer—it's about living better. Alas, we will always be thrown curveballs; and just when we think we know what's coming next, the occasional change-up. We may not be able to do anything about the weather or the State of the Union. But what we *do* have control over are both our own thoughts and the way we act toward others. Yes, each and every one of us, myself absolutely included, needs help coping, whether our issues are large or small, life altering or simply annoying. Each of our lives is an accumulation of the results of a series of choices—the way we think, what we do, and the way we react—to others and outside forces and events—that define our emotional, physical, and spiritual health and well-being. By having climbed our Ladder, you now have the tools that will help break the cycle of negativity, develop a positive, proactive attitude, and rebuild your self-confidence. In another words, you will be able to embrace life more fully than ever.

Going forward, I would like my personal mantra to become yours: I have the Wisdom to accept that I have obstacles to overcome, the Power to adapt to the lifestyle changes I need to conquer them, and the Courage to move on.

I will never forget the words of one survivor: "Just when the caterpillar thinks its life is over, it turns into a butterfly." So with your newfound knowledge it is now time to spread your own wings. Being Better Than Before doesn't mean that we have to change the world. All we need to do is direct a little more positive energy each day toward improving our lives—plus the lives of all those we touch.

So until we meet again, Be Wise! Be Well! Be Better Than Before!

Additional Reading

Allergies, and Awesome You: Believe You Can Get There Too! Dr. Atul N. Shah

The Book of Psychological Truths: A Psychiatrists Guide to Really Good Thinking for Really Great Living, R. Duncan Wallace, M.D.

The Complete Book of Juicing, Revised and Updated: Your Delicious Guide to Youthful Vitality, Michael T. Murray, N.D.

Conversations with the Goddess: Encounter at Petra, Place of Power, Dorothy Atalla

Die Fat or Get Tough: 101 Differences in Thinking Between Fat People and Fit People, Steve Siebold

Eat & Beat Diabetes with Picture Perfect Weight Loss: The Visual Program to Prevent and Control Diabetes, Dr. Howard M. Shapiro

Eat Your Way to Happiness, Elizabeth Somer, M.A., R.D.

Eating Well, Living Better: The Grassroots Gourmet Guide to Good Health and Great Food, Michael S. Fenster, M.D.

The Ecstasy of Surrender: 12 Surprising Ways Letting Go Can Empower Your Life, Judith Orloff, M.D.

Feet First: A Guide to Foot Reflexology, Laura Norman with Thomas Cowan

Finding Happiness: One Man's Quest to Beat Depression and Anxiety and—Finally—Let the Sunshine In, Todd Patkin with Howard J. Rankin, Ph.D.

Get Serious: A Neurosurgeon's Guide to Optimal Health and Fitness, Dr. Brett Osborn

The Hormone Diet: A 3-Step Program to Help You Lose Weight, Gain Strength, and Live Younger Longer, Natasha Turner, N.D.

The Lean: A Revolutionary (and Simple!) 30-Day Plan for Healthy, Lasting Weight Loss, Kathy Freston

Prevent Cancer, Strokes, Heart Attacks and Other Deadly Killers, Vijaya Nair, M.D.

Reiki Energetics: Energetic Theories & Practices for Healing & Wellness, John Kroneck

Sex and Spaghetti Sauce: My Italian Mother's Recipe for Getting Healthy and Getting Busy in Your 50s and Beyond, Carmella Sebastian, M.D., M.S.

Survivorship: Living Well During and After Cancer, Barrie Cassileth, Ph.D.

The Synthesis Effect: Your Direct Path to Personal Power and Transformation, John McGrail, Ph.D.

You Can Heal Yourself: A Guide to Physical and Emotional Recovery After Injury or Illness, Julie Silver, M.D.

Acknowledgments

My sincerest thanks to Spry Publishing's Lynne Johnson, whose leadership and creativity made this book possible, and to Carol Bokas, Project Manager, who guided it to reality. Thanks, too, to Marilyn Knowlton, my writing-style guru. And once again to The Lawyer for his endless hours of unparalleled assistance on this book. To Lisa Rodman, who took my radio show to the next (Be) Major level, and to the wonderful Laurie Huston who now produces it. To both CBS Radio and iHeartRadio Talk for providing me the platforms to reach my devoted listeners across the country and beyond. Thank you, Brittany Hensel, for being with me since the start and so skillfully navigating all of my social media sites. To Lisa Delaney, SVP/Editorial Director of Athlon Media Group, for seeing promise in Better Than Before for a magazine and online column; and the awesome Anna Dickens for continuing to work with me at Spry Living. To Alex Ward of the *New York Times* who long ago started me on my book writing journey. To my editors at *Town & Country* magazine, the *International Herald Tribune, Harper's Bazaar,* The Chopra's Intent.com, She Knows, AARP, and *Cosmopolitan* magazine, to name a few, for providing me the opportunities to research and interview so many amazing experts over the years. To the superb publicists and public relations firms with whom I work who facilitate many of those phenomenal interviews. Special thanks to Natalie Bushaw and her remarkable sons, and to Gabriella McNamara, Johanna J. Ramos-Boyer, and my work-out partner, Emily Tidswell. Finally, my never-ending appreciation to Rachel Thurber for helping me to share her dad's—Raymond Wright—extraordinary legacy to benefit so many, many more. And to the readers of this book whose climb up the rungs will inspire me to take our Better Than Before Ladder to even greater heights. Long Live You!!

Index

Jane Wilkens Michael

Through her nationally syndicated radio show, lifestyle columns, and sports nutrition book, Jane Wilkens Michael has helped millions of readers and listeners become better than before. An innovative program that is designed to enlighten, empower, and improve your everyday life, *Better Than Before* features nine simple lifestyle "Rungs," replete with beauty, health, and wellness advice, that work synergistically to relax, replenish, and rejuvenate the body, mind, and spirit.

Jane began her career creating the monthly "Beauty Talk" column for *Town & Country* magazine, and she has gone on to contribute her columns and articles to an extensive list of renowned publications, newspapers, and websites. Her weekly radio program can be heard on iHeartMedia's iHeartRadio Talk.

Jane is the author of *Breakfast, Lunch and Dinner of Champions*, a book based on an article originally published in the *New York Times. Long Live You!* is her first book with Spry Publishing.